D0845975

US SPECIAL FORCES

US SPECIAL FORCES

PETER MACDONALD

GALLERY BOOKS
An imprint of W.H. Smith Publishers Inc.
112 Madison Avenue
New York, New York 10016

Published by Gallery Books
A Division of W.H. Smith Publishers Inc.
112 Madison Avenue
New York, New York 10016

Produced by
Brompton Books Corp.
15 Sherwood Place
Greenwich, CT 06830

ISBN 0-8317-2674-1

Printed in Hong Kong

10 9 8 7 6 5 4 3 2 1

CONTENTS

PAGE 1: US Marines and helicopter aircrew taking cover in a trench during an artillery barrage on the American base at Khe Sanh, Vietnam. The North Vietnamese siege of Khe Sanh was intended to be the United States' Dien Bien Phu but the Marines held despite repeated attempts to dislodge them.

PAGE 2 (ABOVE LEFT): Paratroopers stand in front of a C-47 aircraft while their kit is unloaded. The Dakota was used by US airborne forces during World War II and Korea.

PAGE 2 (ABOVE RIGHT): US Marines stand in front of their national flag after the successful invasion of Grenada. The Marine Corps played an important role in this short campaign.

PAGE 2 (BELOW LEFT): Dressed in desert camouflage fatigues and armed with M-60 machine guns paratroopers from the United States Rapid Deployment Force await their turn to be airlifted to the exercise area.

PAGE 2 (BELOW RIGHT): Members of an air cavalry troop fan out from an LZ after jumping from their hovering Huey helicopter.

PAGE 3: Armed with a grenade-launcher, a member of the 101st Airborne Division prepares to engage an enemy bunker.

LEFT: A US Army Ranger receives a light for his cigarette after returning from the Dieppe raid in World War II.

INTRODUCTION

ELITE military units have fired the imagination of soldiers and civilians alike for centuries. However, despite catching the eye with specially designed uniforms and insignia, drawing attention with acts of extreme daring and heroism, their exact nature has often been the source of much discussion and debate throughout their existence. The term 'elite' has also been used and misused to describe countless units from numerous countries since the beginnings of military history.

Throughout its history the United States of America has had a series of top-rate military formations, performing vital functions in times of war and, on occasion, in times of comparative peace. The first American unit with the special role and the *esprit de corps* needed by any elite force was raised by the British during the French and Indian Wars in North America during the eighteenth century. Known as Rogers' Rangers, these woodsmen-cum-soldiers fought an effective campaign behind the lines of the French Army and its Indian allies.

In America's early post-colonial history various special formations were created when the need arose. During the Civil War the South raised a number of unorthodox cavalry units which waged effective guerrilla raids against the North. Such units were known variously as 'raiders' or 'marauders,' titles that were to distinguish other formations in World War II.

After the end of the Civil War the United States continued to use specially trained troops in the Indian Wars and in the war against Spain. The United States Marine Corps became a 'traditional' elite, involved in numerous campaigns abroad and was often used as the strong arm of American foreign policy. During World War I it was the Marine Corps which saw much of the fighting in the trenches on the Western Front.

In World War II many new elite units were formed. Rangers were raised along the lines of Britain's Commandos, Marauders fought in the jungles of Burma, and Marine Raiders launched the first amphibious assaults against Japanese-held islands in the Pacific. In addition airborne troops were used for the first time, bringing a number of changes to the traditional arts of warfare. Many of these units were disbanded at the end of the war, only to be needed again in Korea a few years later. American involvement in the Vietnam War brought about a resurgence of interest in elite units. Special operations forces, a new type of elite, played an important role during the war. The army's Special Forces, or 'Green Berets' as they are popularly known, fought a different kind of war, as did the navy's SEALS. Riverine and airmobile operations influenced new battlefield tactics and strategies.

This book charts the history of these and other elite units from the early days of World War II, beginning with the rebirth of the Rangers, to recent missions involving special forces – operations which include the ill-fated Iranian hostage rescue attempt and the later, more successful American invasion of Grenada.

ELITE military units are often formed as a result of a particular need. In some cases the need is to counter a specific enemy threat; in others to attack a certain type of target. The formation of the US Army Rangers came about at a period in World War II when the United States of America and its Allies had suffered a series of humiliating defeats. The Allies were finding it increasingly difficult to come to grips with the enemy on favorable terms, and it was thought that the formation of a special commando-type unit would give the US Army the ability to fight back against a strong and so far successful foe.

The solution to the problem was the formation of an elite, highly trained, aggressive unit – the Rangers. The initial idea came from Brigadier General Lucien Truscott, an experienced US Army officer who was head

Criteria on which the initial selection was based were primarily physical. Volunteers had to be fit and athletic, good swimmers, and capable of maintaining a 60-inch pace on long speed marches. Skills such as mountain climbing and fieldcraft, and the ability to navigate across country were also considered in selecting men for further training. Darby chose likely volunteers from all branches of the US Army's ground forces and consequently recruited men with a diverse range of specialist as well as individual skills. Those chosen by Darby and his team of officers were sent for further selection to Carrickfergus Camp to the north of Belfast, where they underwent two weeks of arduous physical testing. As a result some 500 men passed on to form the basis of the 1st Ranger Battalion.

Like their early counterparts, the Rangers

CHAPTER 1

WORLD WAR II ELITES

of the mission attached to Britain's Combined Operations in 1942. Truscott convinced the US Army Chief of Staff, General George C Marshall, of the need to raise an elite formation similar to Britain's Commandos. The officer chosen to raise and lead this new unit was Major William O Darby, aide-de-camp to the general commanding the US 34th Infantry Division in Northern Ireland.

All elite units, if they are to be successful, require a particularly high standard of volunteer. After carefully selecting a cadre of officers to help him, Darby set about interviewing and selecting the first volunteers from the division's many units. Unit commanders were naturally reluctant to lose some of their best men to the new formation, but with the backing of senior US Army officers, Darby was able to choose the men he wanted without interference, and all those who volunteered were considered for selection.

of World War II operated closely with the British. Within a week of its formation the 1st Ranger Battalion came under the umbrella of Britain's Special Service Brigade and, shortly after, the battalion moved on mass for Commando training at Achnacarry in the northeast highlands of Scotland. Here the volunteers underwent rigorous training, tutored by experienced British Commando instructors. The next month was spent learning a variety of skills including rock climbing and unarmed combat. The lessons were conducted under field conditions, full equipment was carried at all times and live ammunition was used on both the assault and obstacle courses. There were casualties but these were both expected and accepted as training had to be as realistic as possible. In spite of the hardship a strong bond was established between the American Rangers and their British Commando instructors, a relationship based on mutual respect which was to last throughout the war and stood

LEFT: Army Rangers practicing an amphibious landing in Algeria, North Africa in 1942.

the Rangers in good stead when they operated with British units. In fact the Rangers spent more time working alongside the British than any other American unit in the war.

After Achnacarry the battalion was divided into two companies and moved to northern Scotland for amphibious training with the Royal Navy. Meanwhile a detachment of six officers and 44 men was selected to participate in a raid on the heavily defended French port of Dieppe. Darby had wanted to lead the complete battalion but was turned down, and the 50 Rangers who actually took part in the raid were allowed to do so as a token gesture only. The detachment moved to the south coast of England and joined a combined Canadian, British and Free-French force. On 18 August the raiding force, comprising over 6000 troops, set sail in a fleet of 253 vessels of various types. It was the largest raid to be launched during the war and its principal aim was to land a large body of troops to test the German defensive capabilities and, at the same time, try out Allied assault tactics and equipment. In reality Dieppe was less of a raid and more of a small-scale invasion. The 50 Rangers who took part were divided among Nos 3 and 4 Commandos, and the Canadian 2nd Division.

The actual assault proved very costly in

LEFT: Battle-weary troops returning from the Dieppe raid. Although only a token Ranger force was involved in the operation, it was significant in that they were the first US troops to be used in the European theater during World War II.

BELOW LEFT: Brigadier General Truscott being introduced to US Army Rangers by Major William Darby during an inspection at a Commando school in England prior to the Dieppe raid.

ABOVE RIGHT: Heavily laden and equipped with a reserve parachute, a US airborne soldier boards a Dakota prior to the Allied invasion of Normandy.

terms of men and material, with the larger Canadian contingent suffering the most casualties and men taken prisoner. Although a failure the raid led to greater understanding on the part of the Allies on how to mount a successful amphibious assault. For the Rangers who took part it was their baptism of fire. Although the American media, quite naturally, played up the role of the Ranger detachment, the action was nevertheless important to the US Army in general, and the Rangers in particular. It was their first contact with the enemy and they had acquitted themselves

well. One Ranger, Corporal Franklin Koons, became the first US soldier to kill an enemy in Europe during World War II. Awarded the Silver Star, Koons was also decorated with the Military Medal by Britain's Head of Combined Operations, Lord Louis Mountbatten, for his bravery while fighting with No 4 Commando.

Meanwhile the remainder of the battalion completed its amphibious training in the north of Scotland and then moved south to Dundee where, like their Commando counterparts, the Rangers were billeted with civilians in the city. The arrangement proved successful for both parties and Dundee became a second home for the 1st Ranger Battalion. To this day a monument stands just outside the city, erected by the people of Dundee in memory of the Rangers. After leaving Dundee the battalion carried out further amphibious training at Corker Hill near Glasgow before embarking on troopships for North Africa in October. Darby was promoted to lieutenant colonel and led the 1st Battalion throughout the campaign in North Africa.

Initially the 1st Battalion acted as a spearhead for Operation Torch, landing in advance of the US 1st Division and securing the coastal town of Arzew in Algeria on 8 November. The landings went well and the Rangers had little difficulty overcoming the Vichy French defenses. After a period of relative quiet during which exhaustive training was conducted in the local desert, the Rangers boarded a commando ship for an amphibious assault on the island of La Galite. At the last minute the operation was called off and the disappointed Rangers returned to Arzew. More training followed, with special emphasis on night operations. However, the lack of promised action had its effect on morale and a number of men applied for transfers to other units. Things got marginally better with the arrival of new recruits from the recently established Ranger training camps in the United States, and the old hands set about bringing these new men up to the standards set by the Commandos in Achnacarry.

No sooner had this diversion begun than word came to move by air and land to Tebéssa, the main American base in western Tunisia. The battalion was tasked with diverting attention from the Allied troop concentrations building up in the north of the country. To this end the Rangers moved up to Gafsa, 70 miles away, to attack Italian positions in the mountains around El Guettar. The Rangers' training in night operations paid off: their approach march up to the Italian positions went undetected until they were within 50 yards of the enemy. The following attack was particularly aggressive and the Italians paid the price for the Rangers' frustration after months of inactivity. The Italians, belonging to the 10th Bersaglieri Regiment, were soundly defeated. Those who remained were mostly killed in the fierce hand-to-hand fighting that followed the initial assault.

The Rangers wasted no time after their victory. Conscious that they were some miles behind enemy lines and that there was a strong German presence in the immediate area, the Rangers began their withdrawal. Dividing into two groups they moved back toward their own lines under cover of darkness and, in spite of enemy activity, including armored patrols, returned to their positions without further contact with the enemy. The operation against the Italians was a resounding success, but the Ranger battalion soon found itself facing an even more determined enemy in the Afrika Korps. During the following month the Rangers were tasked with acting as a rearguard in the south as the remaining American units pulled back toward the north, where they consolidated a shorter and more effective defensive line.

The first phase of the rearguard action went without mishap and the Rangers withdrew to their second line of defense some distance to the north but still to the south of the main body of friendly forces. It was at this point that plans started to go awry. The orders to move from the second position arrived some four hours late, by which time all the battalion's transport had been withdrawn, leaving the Rangers on their own. Calculating the speed of the enemy advance and his Rangers' ability to move on foot, Darby reckoned that both parties would reach the comparative safety of the main Allied line, some 25 miles to the north, at approximately the same time. The Rangers'

BELOW: A Ranger moves toward the fighting during operations in North Africa, 1943. Fit and lightly equipped the Rangers were capable of moving extremely quickly over difficult terrain.

pace to the Allied line at Dernia was fast and furious, and they made it – but only just. Enemy panzers caught up with them as they entered the foothills around Dernia and their ranging shots landed a mere 50 yards behind the last elements of the rearguard.

There followed several weeks of relative inactivity for the Rangers as they carried out patrols and generally harried the enemy. The direction of the enemy advance shifted to the northwest of Dernia and finally came to a halt at the Kasserine Pass, some eight miles from the Rangers' positions. The tide was about to turn in favor of the Americans and when General George S Patton took command of II Corps, which included both the 1st Armored and 34th Infantry Divisions, the Americans went on the offensive. Receiving orders to retake Gafsa and continue southeast to take the heights around El Guettar, the commander of the 1st Armored Division, General Allen, decided to use the Rangers as his spearhead battalion. The advance to Gafsa was uneventful as the enemy had withdrawn from the town but, as Ranger reconnaissance patrols soon discovered, they had established heavily fortified positions on the high ground to either side of the two roads heading out of the town. The main road from Gafsa to the coastal town of Sfax ran through the El

Guettar Pass, but just before the pass it divided, with the second road taking a more southerly route through a second pass before continuing in a southeasterly direction to the town of Gabes, the largest port in southern Tunisia. The securing of both routes was vital to the success of the American offensive.

Acting on information provided by his own scouts, Darby proposed a plan involving scaling the heights to the rear of the enemy positions, followed by an assault. Darby conducted his own reconnaissance prior to putting his ideas forward to both Allen and Patton. The generals approved, also giving him a further 48 hours to carry out a more detailed reconnaissance and finalize his plans. His scouting patrols came back with information which was both valuable and favorable: the enemy positions were well-placed and heavily defended, with antitank weapons and heavy machine guns protected by artillery directed by well-positioned spotters, but were all forward facing. In choosing the positions the enemy had only considered the possibility of a frontal assault, neglecting the defense of their rear. In addition reconnaissance revealed that the defenders were Italian, and although there were at least six German divisions in the mountains, these troops

BELOW: The first Ranger battalion 'moving up' during the campaign in North Africa in 1943.

were not manning the targeted positions.

On the night of 21 March 1943 the Rangers, supported by a divisional engineer mortar company, began to advance in column toward the Italian positions. Using previously reconnoitered goat tracks the Rangers scaled the mountain and were in position behind the Italians before first light. Calculating that the engineer mortar company, which despite all efforts had lagged behind the main party, would be in position before the Rangers' own mortars had run out of ammunition, Darby decided to begin the attack. As dawn broke the Rangers on the plateau opened fire and attacked the ridge. Within two hours the Italian positions had been overrun and secured, with over 200 prisoners taken.

The Rangers then continued their advance down the hill, taking an 88mm gun position before being halted by a well-sited machine gun. Just as the situation began to look difficult the engineer mortar company, having reached the plateau and despite being exhausted, sited their weapons and opened fire on the enemy machine gun. With just three rounds the mortars knocked it out. With the increased mortar support the Rangers pressed home their attack, knocking out an 88mm battery and a num-

ber of machine-gun posts and clearing the El Guettar heights of the enemy. Within eight hours of starting the attack the Ranger battalion had secured both sides of the pass for the 1st Armored Division. Meanwhile divisional troops had secured the heights above the road to Sfax. The attack had been a spectacular success: tons of ammunition had been captured, together with a large number of field artillery pieces and over 1400 Italian prisoners.

Interrogation of these prisoners revealed that the Germans had moved out of the positions some two days previously and divisional intelligence realized the strong possibility of a German counterattack in the near future. Other reports further indicated that the counterattack was planned for mid-afternoon two days later. This information was more accurate than usual. The enemy assault, comprising three German panzer grenadier and two Italian infantry divisions, began exactly when anticipated. The attack on the 1st Ranger Battalion's positions was carried out by panzer grenadiers supported from the rear by some 60 tanks.

The enemy attacked in extended line across the plain and, despite heavy casualties, kept on attacking. Although the initial advance was broken up within 100 yards of

ABOVE: US Rangers waiting patiently in a barge for the signal that will start the Allied amphibious invasion of Europe.

ABOVE: American Rangers move down a road during the advance toward Pompeii, September 1943.

RIGHT: A demonstration of rock climbing skills at a Commando training center in Scotland. Rangers undertook similar training to Britain's Commandos during the run up to D-Day.

the Ranger positions and the panzer grenadiers withdrew under intense artillery fire, the offensive was by no means over. For the next three days, the panzer grenadiers, reinforced by paratroopers, continued the attack. Despite fierce fighting on both sides (much of which took place at night), and the fact that positions changed hands a number of times, the German assault was finally blunted, if not broken, by the 27th. The Rangers, who had been involved in some of the toughest fighting, were withdrawn from the line and their positions occupied by troops of the 1st Armored Division.

The Battle of El Guettar was a major Allied victory. It lasted 21 days in total, and although the Rangers had been withdrawn to be employed as reserve troops on day six of the battle, they had been instrumental in the American success. The Ranger patrol's initial reconnaissance and the battalion's subsequent scaling of the heights behind the Italian positions were classic Ranger tactics. The 1st Ranger Battalion had performed remarkably well and, in some of the most brutal and bloody fighting in North

Africa, came away with surprisingly few casualties.

After the battle the battalion received orders to move back to Oran in Algeria. Darby was awarded the Distinguished Service Cross by General Patton but turned down the offer to be made up to full colonel. Rather than take over command of an infantry regiment Lieutenant Colonel Darby chose to remain with his Ranger battalion. Patton was not the only senior officer to be impressed by Darby and his Rangers, and the Supreme Allied Commander, General Dwight D Eisenhower, realizing the Rangers' achievements, instructed Darby to raise and train a further four battalions. Using the 1st Battalion as a nucleus for the others, two battalions were formed and trained in Oran while two more were raised in the United States.

The newly formed Ranger battalions were to prove as effective as the 1st Battalion. From mid-1943 onward the 1st, 2nd and 3rd Ranger Battalions were involved in the Allied invasions of Sicily and Italy. Acting as spearhead troops the Rangers were the first ashore in the initial amphibious landings and were in the forefront of the drive up through Italy. They saw action at Salerno and Monte Cassino and at the fateful Battle of Cisterna during the fighting around Anzio, where the 1st and 3rd Battalions were virtually wiped out.

The 2nd and 5th Ranger Battalions went on to take part in the Allied landings in Normandy on D-Day, 6 June 1944. The 2nd Battalion, commanded by Lieutenant Colonel James E Rudder, was tasked with destroying a battery of six German 155mm guns at Pointe du Hoe.

This well-sited battery was in a commanding position with a field of fire covering Omaha Beach to the east and Utah Beach to the northwest. These two beaches were the designated landing areas for 1st, 4th, 29th and 90th Infantry Divisions. The 2nd Battalion divided into three groups. Companies D, E, and F were to scale the high cliffs off the beach with the aid of rocket-projected grapnel hooks and rope ladders, prior to carrying out a frontal assault on the gun positions. Company C was to land farther along the coast at Vierville-sur-Mer, and attack the positions from that direction, while Companies A and B were to be held in reserve together with the whole of the 5th Ranger Battalion.

ABOVE: Bayonet fixed a Ranger leaps into action during a realistic training exercise.

In the event things did not go according to plan. The first Ranger assault group left their transport vessels in landing craft 30 minutes before the rest of the task force. Rough seas swamped two of the Rangers' assault craft and disorientated the guide boat to such an extent that it initially approached the wrong beach. The attacking Ranger force was only a few hundred yards offshore when the mistake was recognized and the landing crew had to run the gauntlet of coastal defenses before reaching their planned objective. The timely support of naval gunfire from two destroyers of the US Navy and Royal Navy enabled most of the landing force to reach the 500-yard stretch of beach beneath the enemy positions. Unfortunately the original plan called for the landing force to bracket the headland directly under the German positions, disembarking on two beaches. The Rangers were fortunate to make landfall at all under the circumstances.

One other piece of luck related to the fact that the commander of the 2nd Ranger Battalion, who had been ordered not to accompany his men, had somehow found himself aboard the lead landing craft. Colonel Rudder took firm control of the situation and Company F began to fight its way up the steep cliffs. Meanwhile the reserve company and the 5th Ranger Battalion landed

LEFT: Rangers practice scaling cliffs on the south coast of England with the aid of small, lightweight ladders. During the Allied invasion the Rangers were to take all their major objectives despite heavy casualties.

on Omaha's Dog Green Beach farther to the east. The 5th Battalion was commanded by Colonel Schneider, an officer who had served under Darby and had considerable experience in amphibious operations. Landing with his battalion on a troop-crowded and somewhat confused beach Schneider approached the 29th Division's deputy commander, General Norman Cota. Instructing the 5th Battalion to clear the beach, taking with them troops belonging to the 116th Infantry, Cota remarked 'Rangers, lead the way,' an instruction which has inspired the Rangers to this day. Schneider ordered his company commanders to attack independently and to meet up at a pre-arranged position to the south of Vierville-sur-Mer. The Rangers of the 5th Battalion and Companies A and B of the 2nd Battalion moved out.

Meanwhile the remainder of the 2nd Battalion had taken the German positions on top of Pointe du Hoe. In spite of heavy casualties Rudder had led his men up the steep cliffs and established a defensive position. The area surrounding the enemy gun positions had been heavily shelled and Rudder ordered his Rangers across the cratered countryside toward the enemy emplacements. They were surprised by the lack of opposition and even more surprised when they discovered only one artillery piece in place, and that had been destroyed by Allied naval gunfire. Convinced that the 155mm battery was still in the area Rudder led his force, now depleted to less than half its original strength, farther inland toward the road between Vierville-sur-Mer and Grandcamp-les-Bains, the Rangers' second objective.

Between the deserted concrete gun emplacements and the road the party of Rangers was reduced still further as it came under enemy fire. A further 15 troops were lost and by the time the remainder reached the road they numbered 37, including Rudder. At this point enemy activity slackened enough to allow two NCOs from Company D to reconnoiter the nearby wood. Here they found the remainder of the enemy battery which was to have been moved back to its original positions after the naval bombardment had ceased. Fortunately the appearance of the Rangers at the base of the cliffs had prevented the Germans from bringing up their guns and engaging the vulnerable Allied shipping offshore. Reinforced that evening by a group of 23 Rangers from the

BELOW: Equipped with life preservers and Bangalore torpedoes, Rangers wait to board the barge that will take them to Normandy.

ABOVE: Lightly equipped US paratroopers move off the drop zone after an early practice drop.

LEFT: Watched by civilian spectators US airborne troops practice on a synthetic trainer during the early stages of World War II.

mandos and Chindits, America's Rangers, Raiders and Marauders, all developed new concepts in warfare, but it was Hitler's Germany, however, that made the first and dramatically successful use of a different type of combat soldier – the airborne trooper.

The German success in mounting airborne assaults in 1940 did not escape the notice of the American General Staff. The strategic use of glider-borne troops at Eben Emael, the deployment of 500 paratroops to capture the Albert Canal intact, and the subsequent successes of German airborne forces in overpowering the defenders of Crete in 1941, convinced the US military that the airborne soldier had an important role to play in World War II.

Although the Allies lagged behind Germany and other Axis powers in the development of airborne forces, an American general had first suggested the formation of a division of paratroopers in World War I but the first unit to be raised specifically for the airborne role was the Parachute Test Platoon. Formed in July 1940, the 50-strong unit was renamed the 1st Parachute Platoon and became the cadre for the 501st Parachute Battalion (PIB). The German successes in airborne operations aroused a great deal of interest and the program advanced steadily. By October 1941 four parachute battalions had been raised – the 501st, 502nd, 503rd and 504th. America's entry into World War II prompted further increases and the original battalions were raised to regimental strength, and were joined by the 505th, 506th, 507th, 508th and 511th Parachute Regiments (PIRs). In August 1942 the 82nd and 101st Airborne Divisions were formed. These large formations incorporated the parachute regiments and also included integral airborne artillery and engineer elements, as well as glider and other specialist units.

This expansion of the US Army's airborne arm continued throughout 1943. Further parachute units were raised, the 513th, 515th and 517th Parachute Regiments, and the 11th, 13th and 17th Airborne Divisions were formed. In addition eight glider-borne infantry regiments were added to the US Army's order of battle.

America's airborne troops received their first combat experience in November 1942 when men of the 509th Parachute Infantry Battalion jumped into North Africa as part of Anglo-American Operation Torch. The 82nd Airborne Division arrived in North Africa in May 1943 and proceeded to train for further combat jumps. The 504th and 505th Parachute Infantry Regiments operated during the invasion of Sicily in July

5th Battalion, Rudder and his men held the position for another two days before being relieved by elements of the 116th Infantry.

The operation was a costly one for the two Ranger battalions. The Ranger companies on Dog Green Beach lost 62 troops out of their complement of 130, while the 5th Battalion and the 2nd Battalion's reserve company lost 135 out of 225 men. But the two battalions played an important role in the D-Day landings. The first mission of the 2nd Battalion had been successful, in traditional Ranger fashion. The 2nd Battalion became known henceforth as 'Rudder's Rangers' named, as had the 1st Battalion before them, after their revered leader. This action during the Allied invasion of Normandy was the last Ranger assault of its type during World War II. As the war in Europe drew to a close the Ranger battalions were disbanded. The 6th Rangers, formed in the Pacific Theater and famous for the rescue of American POWs from Japanese prison camps in the Philippines, was deactivated at the same time. The US Army Rangers were to remain inoperative until America needed them again.

World War II saw the emergence of a number of new and completely novel elite forces which saw service with both the Allied and Axis powers. Britain's Com-

1943, in conjunction with the amphibious landings, and in September these two regiments, together with the 82nd Airborne Division's 509th Parachute Infantry Battalion, conducted a combat jump into southern Italy.

After the landings in Italy the next important offensive on the Allied agenda was the invasion of Normandy. In 1944 the 82nd and 101st Airborne Divisions joined together in Britain to carry out the airborne assault prior to the main amphibious landings on D-Day. On 6 June the two divisions jumped into Normandy to capture certain key points, and carry out operations in advance of the amphibious landing forces pushing inland from the beaches. This successful operation was followed by a second just over a month later when members of the 509th and 551st PIBs, and the 517th PIR, spearheaded the Allied invasion in the south of France. The operation involved 10,000 troops of the 1st Airborne Division commanded by General Fredrick, who were parachuted and airlanded by 535 C-47s and 465 gliders behind the German defenses in the Muy region. Sustaining only slight casualties, less than 200 killed and wounded, the airborne force secured the

approach to the Argens valley, denying the German forces the opportunity to counter-attack the bridgehead in Provence.

After receiving replacements for their losses in Normandy, the 82nd and 101st Airborne Divisions were withdrawn to prepare for the most ambitious and largest airborne operation of World War II. This time their mission was to secure a series of key bridges in Holland, which were vital to the success of a major combined operation involving Montgomery's Second Army. The operation was codenamed 'Market Garden' and its aim was to secure the town of Arnhem ahead of the advance and establish a safe corridor for the main army. The British 1st Airborne Division and the Polish Parachute Brigade were tasked with securing Arnhem and its approaches until relieved by the advancing Second Army. The Second Army's route to Arnhem crossed a number of bridges which had to be captured at the beginning of the battle to ensure overall success. The two American airborne divisions were ordered to secure these bridges.

Major General James Gavin's 82nd Airborne Division parachuted into the area around Grave and Nijmegen without mishap and one of his battalions, having landed

BELOW: A Willis jeep being loaded into a Waco glider in preparation for the Allied landings in Sicily, July 1943.

RIGHT: A British brigadier addressing US airborne troops after the capture of Avola, Sicily, 1943.

FAR RIGHT: General Dwight D Eisenhower talking to US paratroopers just prior to the invasion of Europe, June 1944.

BELOW RIGHT: Dead American paratroopers demonstrate the possible result of deploying lightly equipped airborne troops against heavily armed enemy forces.

ABOVE LEFT: American paratroopers being briefed by their commander prior to emplaning for a drop on Europe.

LEFT: A plane-load of paratroopers reflecting a variety of emotions during a flight over the Channel on their way to France.

ABOVE: The 82nd Airborne Division dropping near Nijmegen, Holland, in September 1944. Unlike their British counterparts, the American paratroopers succeeded in achieving their objectives in Market Garden.

RIGHT: American airborne troops inspect the wreckage of one of their gliders after the Nijmegen operation.

astride the Maas River at Grave, managed to capture the bridge within an hour. Within six hours the remaining battalions had secured a crossing over the Maas-Waal Canal and had advanced as far east as the Reichswald. The opposition was easily overcome and it was not until Gavin sent a battalion farther north, to the Waal bridge at Nijmegen, that his paratroopers encountered German forces in any great strength.

Farther to the south Major General Maxwell Taylor's 101st Airborne Division enjoyed equally rapid success during the initial stages of the drop. Encountering little flak the division landed intact and moved off the drop zones quickly, neutralizing the scattered German forces they came across and capturing the vital bridges over the Zuid Willems Vaart Canal at Veghel. Although these bridges were captured intact, the Wilhelmina Canal bridge at Zon was destroyed before the US paratroopers reached it. Despite this setback a parachute infantry regiment successfully crossed the canal and secured the far bank, allowing engineering work to begin. The regiment then moved south into Eindhoven and began to clear the way for the Second Army's armored thrust. By nightfall the leading elements of the British armor had met up with the American paratroopers. The corridor toward Arnhem was now open as far as Nijmegen.

Meanwhile at Nijmegen Gavin's 82nd Airborne Division was encountering problems in capturing the vital bridge over the Waal. The planned dawn attack on the bridge had to be postponed after a German counterattack from the Reichswald overran the landing zones for the division's gliderborne artillery and reserve infantry elements. A fierce battle ensued and the landing zones were retaken just in time to allow the gliders, already delayed for two hours by bad weather, to land in relative safety. The second wave of reinforcements was prevented from landing the following day due to heavy fog, and when Gavin was joined by the Grenadier Guards, spearheading the British advance, he was under so much pressure from the Germans and from his lack of reserves that he was only able to allocate one of his three regiments for a combined attack on the bridges over the Waal. Successive attacks by this regiment, supported by tanks of the Grenadier Guards, were repeatedly beaten off. The German defensive positions held and the German commander was so confident of his troops' ability to hold off the attacks that he ordered the road and rail bridges to be left standing.

A new Allied approach was necessary. The 504th PIR attempted a river assault in the early afternoon at a point a mile downstream from the bridge. Using canvas storm boats brought up by engineers, the regiment launched the craft into the fast-flowing river under heavy fire. Less than half of the first wave made it to the opposite bank but they managed to establish and maintain a small bridgehead. Breaking out of the bridgehead in the late afternoon, the airborne troops secured the northern side of the railroad bridge and moved on to engage the defenders of the road bridge. At this point the Guards, seeing the US paratroopers on the northern side of the rail bridge, mounted a successful assault on the German defenders on the southern side. While Gavin's two remaining PIRs held off the German forces in the Reichswald, the Guards' armor attacked the bridge. Of the four tanks that succeeded in reaching the German positions on the southern side, two were immediately knocked out by concealed antitank weapons positioned among the structure's heavy steel girders. Despite these losses the remaining two managed to reach the comparative safety of the northern side and link up with the paratroopers. An hour later the crossing point spanning the Waal was secure and the way forward was open to the Allies.

BELOW: Hailed as liberators by local Dutch civilians US troops moving forward unopposed after their success at Nijmegen.

RIGHT: Members of the 82nd Airborne Division warm themselves round a fire somewhere in the Ardennes prior to the German offensive.

BELOW: The faces of US paratroopers display intense fatigue after heavy fighting during the Battle of the Bulge, as the Ardennes offensive became known.

The way to Arnhem had been opened, allowing the armored spearhead of XXX Corps, which comprised the leading element of the Second Army, to advance toward the British paratroopers and glider-borne units trying desperately to hold out in the beleaguered town. The operation to capture the bridge at Nijmegen by the Guards Armored and 82nd Airborne Divisions was one of the most dashing and hard-fought actions of the war. General Dempsey, the man responsible for the Second Army's operations, met Gavin after the battle. He is reported to have said, 'I am proud to meet the commander of the greatest division in the world today!' Dempsey did not make an idle compliment, the American airborne, especially the 82nd, had fought brilliantly.

The British 1st Airborne Division was decimated at Arnhem. It was truly 'a bridge too far.' The American divisions had fared better and the 82nd and 101st were pulled back from the front lines. The war was not yet won and the 101st Airborne Division, together with the 82nd, was committed to battle again in support of the American troops countering the Ardennes offensive. The battle for Bastogne, in which the 101st Airborne Division successfully blunted the German onslaught, became one of the most

ABOVE LEFT: US paratroopers watch as a British glider comes into land during operations north of the Rhine toward the end of the war.

LEFT: Horses, pressed into service as ammunition carriers, follow behind the tanks as units of the 82nd Airborne advance through Belgium.

ABOVE: Paratroopers landing on a DZ held by US Marines during operations in the Pacific, July 1944.

famous engagements in American military history. The Battle of the Bulge was finally won and the airborne divisions played no small part in the hard-fought victory.

The final large-scale American parachute deployment to take place in the European Theater occurred in March 1945 when the 17th Airborne Division, newly arrived from America via Britain, jumped into Wesel. The town of Wesel is in Germany and the 17th Airborne Division's mission was vital to the success of Operation Varsity, in which the Allies crossed the Rhine into the German heartland. World War II was coming to a close.

While the 82nd, 101st and 17th Airborne Divisions saw action in Europe, the 13th Airborne Division was under training in the United States, and the 11th Airborne Division was in combat in the Pacific. In September 1943 the 503rd PIR, part of the 11th Airborne Division, carried out the first major parachute deployment in the Pacific with a jump into New Guinea. This was followed by a jump by the same regiment on to Noemfoor Island in July 1944. The 503rd parachuted into action for their third and final time, together with the 511th Parachute Infantry Regiment, in February 1945. The 511th PIR jumped in over Luzon while the

503rd jumped into Corregidor. The latter was a classic parachute deployment to capture a defended island and was the last American airborne operation to take place until the Korean War, some five years later.

The six Ranger Battalions initially raised by Colonel Darby in the European Theater during World War II were the first true Rangers of their era. However there was a second wartime unit to which today's US Army Rangers owe their origins – a unit designed exclusively for jungle operations in India, Burma and China. Its title was the 5307th Composite Unit (Provisional) but became better known as 'Merrill's Marauders' after its commander, Brigadier General Frank D Merrill.

As a result of the Quebec Conference in August 1943 it was decided to form a specialist force able to take the war to the Japanese in India and Burma. Like the Rangers in Europe, which were formed as a result of the Quebec Conference, this new unit was created with a specific purpose in mind, and was the first American ground combat unit to inflict casualties on the enemy in its particular theater of operations.

In 1943 the war in the East was not going well for the Allies. Under the command of an innovative British officer, Orde Wingate, volunteers were formed into the Long Range Penetration Force. Known as 'Chindits,' these troops carried out their first

ABOVE: A member of Merrill's Marauders cleaning a 60mm mortar during the Burma campaign, April 1944.

LEFT: Armed with a flamethrower and Thompson sub-machine guns, members of the 5307th Composite Unit (Provisional) advance on a bunker.

ABOVE: Soldiers relax at the side of a jungle trail during Merrill's advance through Burma. Mules are being used to carry some of the troops' heavier equipment.

operation in northern Burma in 1943. Casualties were high, but a number of important lessons were learnt about jungle warfare and extended patrols, and the importance of air support and resupply in such operations.

The US War Department began to recruit volunteers for a similar unit in September 1943. The original call for volunteers for the new formation, designated Galahad Force, did not produce the expected results. It had been hoped that experienced troops from General Douglas MacArthur's command would come forward but in the event Galahad Force recruited from different sources. The officer responsible for organizing the 5307th Composite Unit (Provisional), which composed Galahad Force, was General George C Marshall. Marshall requested and received 300 volunteers of a high standard of fitness and aptitude from the southwest Pacific area, 700 from the south Pacific, and 1000 from the Caribbean Defense Command and from the US Army in the United States.

The volunteers from the Caribbean had been stationed in tropical areas, mostly in Panama and the West Indies and, together with men drawn from units based in the US,

formed two battalions under the command of Colonel Charles Hunter. These two battalions left San Francisco by troopship in late September to pick up the south Pacific volunteers from New Caledonia before proceeding to Brisbane, where the southwest Pacific recruits boarded. After docking at Perth to take on fuel and supplies the troopship sailed to Bombay. On landing, Colonel Hunter reported to General Stilwell who ordered training to begin immediately. The 5307th was organized into three battalions each consisting of two regimental combat teams and an HQ and support element, comprising a Command Post Group and a Rear Supply Base.

Under British instructors from Wingate's Chindits, the 5307th began intensive training in long-range penetration techniques. The unit began to take shape. Volunteers had been drawn from a wide range of units and initially included more than the normal quota of undesirables. Pressed for men a number of unit commanders had, perhaps understandably, reacted negatively and offered up drunks, derelicts and guardhouse detainees. However it would be naive to assume that all the potential jungle fighters

would naturally conform to the disciplines imposed by more conventional soldiering. As the training neared completion in late January 1944 the members of the 5307th found themselves with a stronger unit identity, partly due to the rigors of the arduous training they had undergone, and partly due to the arrival earlier that month of their new commander. Brigadier General Frank D Merrill took charge on 8 January and 'Merrill's Marauders' were assigned to General Joseph Stilwell's command in northern Burma.

General 'Vinegar Joe' Stilwell was a hard taskmaster. During the spring and summer of 1944 he employed Merrill's command to spearhead the drive to recover northern Burma and clear the way for the construction of a road between India and China. Conditions during the campaign were appalling. Galahad Force marched 500 miles and by late April almost all of the men were suffering from dysentery, malaria or malnutrition, or in some cases all three. After several actions in northern Burma Stilwell committed Merrill and his Marauders to breaking the stalemate at the airfield at Myitkyina on the Irrawaddy River. The attack soon bogged down and took on the attributes of a siege. Together with the Chindits and Nationalist Chinese troops,

Merrill's three understrength battalions were soon in a pathetic condition. The area around the airfield, held with grim determination by the Japanese, resembled a scene from the battlefields of World War I. Illness was so rife that the men of one company cut the seats out of their trousers. The intense fighting took its toll, with one undernourished company commander passing out three times in one day. Merrill himself suffered two heart attacks and had to be evacuated. The force was severely depleted: Galahad had been sent into the field without adequate medical services and casualty evacuation procedures. Aircraft bringing in fresh troops from the United States took out some of the more severely injured but conditions were so gruesome that half the reinforcements became pyschiatric casualties within 24 hours of their arrival.

In late summer the remnants of Merrill's Marauders were withdrawn from the line. Stilwell had kept them in battle far beyond their limit of effectiveness. Wingate had reckoned on a 90-day limit for troops operating in jungle conditions, and Merrill's Marauders had been in constant combat for considerably longer than that. Battle casualties and sickness had reduced the 5307th to a third of its original strength. In August it was redesignated the 475th

LEFT: Marauders move into the jungle on an operation.

Infantry Regiment, becoming part of the newly formed 5332nd Brigade, a unit tasked with conducting deep penetration operations. Known as the 'Mars Task Force,' the brigade began operations on the China-India road in November 1944 and a month later the 475th deployed to the Tongwa-Mo sector where it put down Japanese opposition in the area. Fighting continued up to February 1945 when the Japanese broke contact and withdrew southwards. In late March the brigade moved to China where it became responsible for equipping, organizing and training of some 36 American-sponsored Nationalist Chinese divisions. It was a role to which the former Marauders were well suited, having operated closely with the Chinese 22nd and 38th Divisions during the previous year.

The 475th Infantry Regiment was disbanded in China on 1 July 1945. A month later it was reactivated and renamed the 75th Infantry Regiment, and assigned to the US Army command on Okinawa, where it remained until being disbanded once again in March 1956. Throughout their time in Burma and the Far East the Marauders, and their subsequent derivatives, acquitted themselves well. Their efforts, as they fought their way to the Irrawaddy River, and

their tenacity during the long battle for Myitkyina airfield, earned them a place in the history of modern elites.

While the US Army Rangers, with the exception of the 6th Battalion, concentrated their efforts on the war in Europe, and while Merrill's Marauders fought in the jungles of Burma, there was a third more traditional elite formation fighting America's war in the Pacific. Other specialist combat units, inspired and initially trained by experienced British instructors, were formed as a direct result of World War II. These units belonged to the US Army and were mostly, as was the case with Merrill's 5307th Composite Unit (Provisional), essentially temporary in nature. At a time when the armed forces of the United States of America consisted of the United States Army (including the Army Air Force) and the United States Navy, one organization stands out among all other fighting arms – the US Marine Corps (USMC).

The United States Marines Corps has a distinct identity. Although the organization comes under the Department of the Navy, the Corps is an independent service with its own commandant, who is a member of the Joint Chiefs of Staff. America, traditionally a maritime nation, formed the USMC in 1775 and it became part of the permanent establishment by Act of Congress in 1775. Initially tasked with providing certain navy ships with snipers and boarding parties the Corps' responsibilities grew to incorporate the security of shore bases as well. In 1834 separate companies were formed to serve both at sea and on land, giving the corps the unusual distinction of serving under either the army or the navy, dependent on the particular mission.

During the nineteenth century the Marine Corps became synonymous with active service overseas in support of America's foreign policies. In World War I the Corps deployed to France to fight in the trenches. At the war's end the Corps had grown to a strength of 76,000 men, some 32,000 of whom had served in France. Out of this total, 2459 had been killed or were missing in action and 11,366 were casualties.

In the period between the two world wars the Marines, like the other services, had been reduced in strength. When World War II began the Corps numbered some 18,000 men and was increased to 25,000 on orders of President Franklin D Roosevelt. The following year some 5000 Marine Reserves were mobilized, defensive battalions sent to a number of Pacific islands, and the 1st and later the 2nd Marine Divisions formed. After the Japanese bombing of the Pacific Fleet at

BELOW: Dug into secure defensive positions overlooking the enemy, two platoons await the order to move forward.

Pearl Harbor on 7 December 1941, and the subsequent bombing of Midway, Johnston and Palmyra, Guam was invaded on the 8th. The Japanese landing force comprised some 6000 troops; the Marine garrison some 130 men. The war had started for the Corps.

By the late spring of 1942 the United States had suffered a number of reversals. The Japanese offensive in the south Pacific had captured most of New Guinea, as well as several of the Solomon Islands, including Guadalcanal. The loss of the latter island was particularly unfortunate as a strategically important airfield was being constructed on it at the time it was taken. Australia and New Zealand, with their armies fighting in North Africa, became vulnerable to Japanese invasion.

At a time when the situation looked more and more desperate for America and her Allies the US Navy achieved two victories which were to set the stage for the Marine offensive in the Pacific. A US task force intercepted a Japanese fleet headed for Port Moresby and in a four-day carrier aircraft battle, succeeded in blocking the enemy push to the southwest. In addition US naval intelligence had broken the Japanese naval codes and knew of their plan to conduct a carrier attack on the beleaguered base at Midway. A fierce air-to-air and air-ship engagement ensued. During a two-day battle around Midway the Japanese lost four carriers and most of their aircraft. The threat to Hawaii ended and the Marines swung into action.

Spearheading many Marine operations in the Pacific Theater were specially formed Raider units. Created in 1942 at the urging of Roosevelt, the Raider battalions were, in a sense, a counterpart to Britain's Commandos. Although many regular Marine officers were unhappy about creating what they saw as an elite within an elite, the Raider concept had presidential endorsement. Roosevelt's son, James, a Marine reserve officer, served with one of the Raider battalions, and the idea was approved. The first major Allied amphibious operation began in early August 1942 with landings on Guadalcanal and surrounding islands.

Prior to the main landings, the 1st Raider Battalion, led by Lieutenant Colonel Merritt Edson, landed on Tulagi and defeated the Japanese defenders, killing some 500. As the 1st Marine Division established a beachhead on the main island of Guadalcanal and drove inland to capture the airfield, two companies of the 2nd Raider Battalion carried out a raid on the Japanese at Makin Island. Over 200 raiders, commanded by

Lieutenant Colonel Evans Carlson, were landed successfully by submarine and attacked the Japanese garrison. 'Carlson's Raiders' acquitted themselves well against a superior enemy and at the same time justified the Raider idea.

After the raid on Tulagi Island, the 1st Raider Battalion deployed to Guadalcanal in support of the already established landing force. There then followed a classic case of the misuse of specialist units when the 1st and later the 2nd Raider Battalions were employed in a more traditional role – that of sustained ground combat. In early September 'Edson's Raiders' undertook a flanking attack on Japanese lines of communication, destroying a number of supply dumps, and later that month about 400 Raiders from the 1st Battalion successfully defeated a counterattack by a Japanese force numbering some 1800 troops. In mid-November the 2nd Raider Battalion left the Guadalcanal defensive perimeter and mounted a long-range fighting patrol. In a march that spanned a total of 150 miles 'Carlson's Raiders' fought a running battle with the Japanese 228th Infantry Regiment, killing an estimated 500 enemy at a cost of 16 Marines killed and 18 wounded. The battalion returned to the main Marine force after over a month of continuous combat, tired but intact.

The Marine Raider concept itself remained intact until January 1944 despite efforts by both the army and the navy to gain control over it. In total, four Raider battalions were raised, and a Raider regiment, which worked closely with the Marine Para-

BELOW: Lieutenant Colonel Evans F Carlson (left) being congratulated after the success of the Makin Island raid. President Roosevelt's son, James, also a Raider, looks on.

ABOVE: Landing craft dropping men of the 2nd Raider Battalion onto a beach during amphibious operations in Guadalcanal.

RIGHT: Carlson, US Marine Corps, the main force behind the Marine Raider concept, pictured during a brief visit to Washington, May 1944.

chute Regiment, was formed. In June 1943 the Raider regiment and Edson's 1st Raider Battalion operated with army units in New Georgia. Later joined by the 4th Raider Battalion, the combined force's total casualties after two months comprised half the formation's original strength. Neither the Raider regiment nor the 1st Raider Battalion were to see action as independent units again.

The 2nd and 3rd Raider Battalions went into combat during the amphibious landings on Bougainville in the northern Solomon Islands. These landings were conducted in September/November 1943 by the 3rd Marine Division. Bougainville was a larger island than Guadalcanal and was defended by a garrison of 35,000 men. Fierce fighting ensued. One month later the Marine Corps secured the island, at a cost of 1841 casualties. By this stage in the Pacific the Raiders were essentially employed as standard Marine units. The four Raider battalions were incorporated into the 4th Marine Regiment to replace its losses in the Philippines, and the 5th and 6th Raider Battalions were withdrawn from operational planning. The Raider training facility at Camp Pendleton was closed down and the Raiders ceased to exist.

The Raiders had however proved themselves. The battalions had been composed of specially selected and highly trained volunteers, and Raider commanders were

allowed certain leeway in the planning, preparation and execution of their missions. They had caught the notice of the Marine Corps and fired the imagination of the American public. The Raiders' commanders had developed a certain *esprit de corps*, and many of them enjoyed further military successes – Colonel Carlson went on to become a brigadier general and Colonel Edson went on to win the Medal of Honor before retiring as a major general.

AS World War II was ending in the Pacific and the Allied powers were looking forward to peace, the seeds for the conflict in Korea were already being sown. In August 1945 an Allied agreement laid down that the Japanese forces to the north of the 38th Parallel in Korea would surrender to the advancing Russian armies, and those Japenese to the south of the divide would give themselves up to the US forces. The 38th Parallel became, in effect, a political frontier.

The Republic of Korea (ROK) was established in the south in August 1947, after diplomatic efforts failed to unify the country. The ROK was supported by the US, while in the north the Democratic Peoples Republic of Korea created the North Korean Army (NKA) under Soviet advisership. In a surprise offensive which began in late June launched a massive counteroffensive. China committed around 180,000 troops to the attack and the Korean War began in earnest.

The end of World War II had brought about a number of changes within the US Army. Many of the elite formations, such as the Army's Rangers and Merrill's Marauders, had been disbanded, and the Marine Corps' Raider battalions had been dissolved or amalgamated. Congressional cutbacks in the strength of the US Army had severely reduced its airborne forces, and the 13th, 17th and 101st Airborne Divisions had been deactivated. The 82nd Airborne Division had returned to the United States in January 1946 and lost its airborne role in 1948. Many military commanders thought of paratroopers as a thing of the past and the 82nd was redesignated as a regular army unit.

CHAPTER 2

KOREAN INTERLUDE

1950 an NKA force, comprising seven infantry divisions and an armored brigade, attacked the South and advanced toward Seoul. The US and United Nations were unable to deal with the crisis by political measures and it soon became obvious that military means were required. Seoul fell on 28 June, and the NKA then pushed US and ROK forces into a confined area around Pusan, 200 miles to the south of Seoul, by early August. The situation had become critical. The US X Corps began landing troops at Inchon, 150 miles to the north of the Allied perimeter at Pusan and a few miles from Seoul, on 15 September. US and ROK forces within the Pusan perimeter pushed northward and succeeded in linking up with the X Corps later in the month. Seoul was liberated and the NKA was effectively cut in half. Continuing the advance UN troops again moved northward and succeeded in occupying two-thirds of North Korea by late November, just before China

The 11th Airborne Division had fared better than its counterparts. After the Luzon campaign the division was preparing for the invasion of Japan when World War II ended. Together with the 27th Infantry Division, the 11th Airborne was tasked with the military occupation of Japan. The 187th Glider Infantry Regiment, which had fought in the Pacific, had become parachute trained and remained in Japan after the 11th Airborne Division left in 1949. At the outbreak of the Korean War the 187th Airborne Infantry Regiment as it had become known, was retitled the 187th Airborne Regimental Combat Team (RCT) and came under the command of Colonel Frank S Bowen. Post-World War II reductions in airborne forces had in fact benefited the 187th. As other units were disbanded the 187th had gained a number of veterans from the 82nd and 101st Airborne Divisions. Changes in the airborne concept had also led to the formation of the 8081st Quartermaster Airborne Air Supply and

LEFT: Marines pause in front of a burning tobacco warehouse during the push through to the heart of Inchon, Korea. The 1st Marine Division spearheaded the American advance.

Packaging Company which, together with the 187th RCT's integral Quartermaster Parachute Maintenance Detachment, was to prove invaluable to US and other UN troops fighting in Korea.

The Regimental Combat Team's initial involvement in the Korean conflict began with the drive north from the Pusan perimeter. Tasked with carrying out an airdrop the 187th's 1st Battalion was diverted to Kimpo airfield where they came under sniper fire on landing. Moving to Suwon they were given the task of clearing the Kimpo peninsula between the Han River and the coast, held at that time by an enemy force of around 3000 men. The NKA force comprised units broken up or left behind in the wake of the American advance north to Inchon. Fighting continued for some time, occasionally heavy, but mostly sporadic. At one point however, Company A of the 1st Battalion encountered strong resistance which could only be overcome with the support of naval gunfire. By the end of the operation in the peninsula the 187th Regimental Combat Team had succeeded in killing or capturing all but 10 percent of the enemy.

Further plans were made to employ the paratroopers in airborne operations in early October but the speed of the US and UN forces' advance to the north was too rapid. No sooner was a drop zone decided on than it was overrun by friendly forces. Then in mid-October the 187th was given its chance. Intelligence reports suggested that the North Koreans, who had slowed their withdrawal and were beginning to make a stand, were moving senior officials and American prisoners by train to the Sukchon-Sunchon area. The RCT was tasked with intercepting and capturing the train. The 1st Battalion's primary mission was to capture

the town of Sukchon and hold the area to the north. The 2nd Battalion was to take the town of Sunchon and to capture the train and its passengers, while the 3rd Battalion was to drop just outside Sukchon, block the road and railroad, and prevent enemy movement between Pyongyang and the Sukchon-Sunchon area.

In the event the drop was delayed for a day because of bad weather, the curse of all airborne operations, and the train had already left Pyongyang for Sunchon when the paratroopers finally emplaned. In all 73 C-119 aircraft from the 314th Troop Carrier Wing, together with 40 C-47s of the 21st Wing, were used in the operation. The early afternoon drops were conducted successfully, under cover of American fighter aircraft, and 1470 paratroopers and 74 tons of equipment were landed. The battalions met with little resistance and by evening Colonel Bowen reported back that the team had achieved all its primary objectives with relatively few losses.

During the second day the 1st and 3rd Battalions continued their attacks and, although they were in place across an NKA defensive line, they only uncovered stores, encountering few enemy troops. As they continued across the low ground and into the hills resistance stiffened and the paratroopers came under enemy mortar, artillery and tank fire. One of the 3rd Battalion's companies was attacked by an NKA battalion on having taken the town of Opari, and was engaged by 40mm guns and 120mm mortars. Without heavy support weapons of their own the company lost over 90 men before being forced to withdraw from the town. The NKA forces did not exploit their advantage and drew back from the town. Additional UN troops were beginning to

LEFT: Landing craft of the 1st Marine Division head for Inchon harbor during the American invasion of the port.

ABOVE: Members of the 187th Regimental Combat Team parachuting into enemy territory during operations in Korea. The aim of the operation was to flank the communist forces in that area. It was successful.

move up to positions held by the RCT and the enemy was being encircled.

One objective remained. The train from Pyongyang had been missed due to the delay in jumping caused by the bad weather. On the third day a 2nd Battalion patrol came across the bodies of 75 US prisoners and recovered 18 wounded survivors of an NKA massacre perpetrated two days previously. The 187th dug in and continued to send out fighting patrols. Enemy activity increased and the battalions came under attack. The North Koreans had a tremendous advantage in terms of numbers, but the paratroopers held on tenaciously. Relief came in the form of armored elements of the British 27th Brigade, which advanced through the paratroopers' positions, driving the enemy before them. The fighting had

been particularly intense and bloody. The 3rd Battalion alone had accounted for 805 North Koreans killed and had captured a further 681. They had engaged the NKA's 239th Infantry Regiment and destroyed it. The 187th Regimental Combat Team's first major airborne operation had been a resounding success.

The remarkable achievement of America's airborne forces during the first major UN offensive in Korea did not pass unnoticed. The 18th Airborne Division was reactivated at Fort Bragg, North Carolina. After the UN withdrawal from the north following the Chinese offensive the 187th established a camp at the Taegu airstrip. In February 1951 the 187th was joined by two Ranger companies, the 2nd and the 4th, and a parachute training program was under-

taken to introduce the Rangers and the attached quartermaster elements to the art of military parachuting.

The army's Rangers had been reactivated when the need for 'marauder companies' was recognized by US military commanders. The mountainous terrain of much of Korea lent itself to small units specially trained in infiltration and sabotage techniques. The Ranger Training Center (Airborne) at Fort Benning, Georgia, was activated and by November 1950 four Ranger companies had graduated after the first six-week course. A second cycle followed and in January 1951 the eight Ranger companies completed a four-week cold weather and mountain training course at Camp Carson, Colorado. In total six Ranger companies, the 1st, 2nd, 3rd, 4th, 5th and 7th were committed to the conflict in Korea. Assigned to the Eighth Army the Rangers operated under divisional, and occasionally corps, control. They conducted raids and reconnaissance patrols, led assaults, carried out ambushes and were employed as regimental reserves tasked with counterattacking enemy units when required. In many cases the Rangers were misused by commanders who did not understand their value as specialist troops, a problem encountered too often by elite units of this nature.

The men of the 2nd and 4th Ranger Companies fared better than their fellows. Attached to the 187th Regimental Combat Team the Rangers took part in the airborne combat jump into Munsan-Ni in March 1951. The aim of the operation was to land behind the forward lines of the North Korean 19th Division and hold the position until relieved by an armored thrust. The idea behind the operation was to cut off retreating NKA units, and the specific task of the two Ranger companies was to move southeast of the RCT's drop zone and capture the town of Munsan-Ni itself. This airborne operation, the second for the 187th and the first for the two Ranger companies, was a success.

Despite casualties, mainly among the 1st and 2nd Battalions during the initial stages of the battle, the Rangers succeeded in taking their objective. The success of the Rangers, unlike that of the airborne RCT, was not matched in the field of military politics as it had been on the field of battle. After returning to their parent units in April the Rangers found themselves under threat of deactivation and this was duly carried out in July 1951. Operations behind enemy lines for non-oriental troops were considered too difficult, especially when such operations demanded that covert tactics be adopted. Additionally the Ranger manning slots were to be used for the formation of a new elite, the Special Forces. The war in Korea became static in nature, only ending in late July 1953 with the signing of a long-overdue peace treaty.

ABOVE: Marines landing at Inchon, 15 September 1950.

ABOVE RIGHT: Marines deploying from a helicopter during Operation Summit. The US Marine Corps pioneered the use of helicopters for airlanding and resupply missions.

RIGHT: A heavily armed Marine fireteam on their way to battle. Although in their infancy, helicopter operations steadily developed and were used with increasing frequency toward the final stages of the war in Korea.

THE US Army Special Forces is one of the most famous elite military formations in the world. Formed with the activation of the 10th Special Forces Group (Airborne) at Fort Bragg, North Carolina, in June 1952, the Green Berets, as this new unit was to become known, came into being before the end of the Korean War. Under the command of Colonel Aaron Bank the group was to pioneer US unconventional warfare techniques. Bank had previously set up the army's Psychological Division and, together with its section chief at the Pentagon, Brigadier General Robert A McClure, he realized the need for a unit specially trained in guerrilla warfare. This unit would be capable of countering communist forces in the Third World.

The concept of a special unit trained in unconventional warfare was not a new one were credited with over 5500 Japanese killed and a further 10,000 wounded.

After the Allied invasion of Normandy the OSS also operated three-man teams which parachuted behind enemy lines to organize and arm resistance groups, harass the enemy and cut lines of communication. Known as 'Jedburgh' or 'Jed' teams, these small units comprised two officers, one from the OSS or its British counterpart the SOE; one officer from the country in which the team was operating; and a US Army or British radio operator. The SOE (Special Operations Executive) and the OSS were pioneers in the field of irregular warfare. They proved that small parties of specially selected and highly trained personnel could operate behind the lines, obtain vital strategic intelligence, organize resistance movements and carry out a successful guer-

CHAPTER 3

ELITES IN VIETNAM

LEFT: Special Forces personnel instructing South Vietnamese troops in the use of the 40mm grenade-launcher prior to America's main involvement in Vietnam. The Green Berets are part of an A-Team from 7th Special Forces Group.

to the American government. During World War II the Office of Strategic Services (OSS) was established to undertake such missions. Under the command of General William Donovan, the OSS recruited army officers, industrialists and academics who were placed into various divisions within the organization. Among the largest of these sub-divisions were the OSS operational groups, composed of 34-man teams. These detachments were infiltrated into enemy-occupied countries to coordinate resistance and to train guerrillas. During the war there were over 80 of these operational detachments, and groups were parachuted into a number of European countries, including France, Italy, Greece, Yugoslavia, and southeast Asia. One such unit, Detachment 101 operated in Burma where it trained and equipped 9000 Kachin tribesmen. Detachment 101 and its Kachin 'Rangers' conducted some of the most successful unconventional operations of the war and

rilla war against the enemy.

The OSS, like many other unconventional and highly specialized formations, was disbanded at the end of World War II. When Bank, a former OSS officer and Jedburgh team member, created the 10th Special Forces Group (Airborne) he selected men with previous experience, soldiers who had served with Ranger or airborne units, or other special operations units. In addition Bank was able to recruit a number of foreign nationals, including displaced persons from communist-occupied countries. This gave the Special Forces a pool of foreign-language speakers to draw on for its operations. After initial selection the volunteers for the 10th SF Group underwent a rigorous training program with much emphasis placed on individual skills. Apart from normal infantry training the recruits had to pass specialist courses which included communications, demolitions, operational intelligence and medicine. Escape and evasion techniques were practised in realistic exercises, mountain and winter warfare was taught in Colorado, and amphibious training was undertaken in the swamps and coastal areas of Florida. By the end of 1952 the 10th SF Group was trained and ready for operational deployment.

The years between 1953 and 1961 were fairly quiet for the Special Forces. In early 1953 a detachment was sent to Korea where it acted in an advisory capacity to the Far East Command, and later the same year, half the group moved to West Germany as part of the US commitment to that country in the light of the worsening relations with the Soviet Union. The remainder of the group stayed at Fort Bragg and was renamed the 77th Special Forces Group (Airborne). From 1956 onward the Special Forces became increasingly involved in southeast Asia. Detachments conducted training missions throughout the sub-continent and formed the nucleus of a new group, 1st SF Group (Airborne), activated on Okinawa. The 77th SF Group was retitled the 7th and, together with the 1st, deployed teams to Nationalist China, Thailand and Vietnam. Their experience in southeast Asia was to stand the Special Forces in good stead during the forthcoming conflict.

The year 1961 brought expansion and change to the Special Forces after a visit to Fort Bragg by President John F Kennedy drew attention to the unit. Impressed by what he saw, Kennedy ordered the expansion of the Special Forces and the formation of four new groups. He also authorized the green beret, up until then unofficial, to be worn by all SF personnel. The 5th SF Group was formed in 1961 and in 1963 three further groups, the 3rd, 6th and 8th, were formed. The commitment to southeast Asia was stepped up and further training deployments were undertaken.

The Special Forces' rapid expansion brought problems, however, and the extremely high standards previously demanded of volunteers were lowered. Despite this setback the Special Forces Training Center managed to produce good-quality troops, soldiers of a higher caliber than those in most US military formations, and although the drop in standards was detrimental to the Special Forces, its newfound notoriety was not. Expansion brought with it a number of benefits, including a much-increased budget. More money meant better training, and more funds improved both individual and team skills. In addition an exchange program enabled US soldiers to attend training courses run by their counterparts in other countries.

During this period training teams from the various groups undertook a variety of different deployments around the world, acting on the whole as military advisers to foreign governments and tutoring their security forces in counterinsurgency techniques. In addition each SF Group was assigned individual areas of responsibility. The 1st and 5th SF Groups were assigned to southeast Asia, the 3rd to Africa, the 6th to the Middle East, and the 7th and 8th to Central and South America. Because of its geographical position and the complexity of its politics, Latin America was, at this time, considered of vital strategic importance. It was in southeast Asia, however, that the US Special Forces were to become most heavily involved. The conflict in Vietnam was escalating.

From 1960 onward the guerrilla war in South Vietnam was on the increase. In rural areas village chiefs and local administrators were being assassinated at a rate of 15 or more per week, while other local leaders were defecting and some villages were actively supporting Viet Cong (VC) groups. In addition there were an estimated 7000

BELOW: Brigadier General William Yarborough, US Army Special Forces, greets John F Kennedy during the president's visit to the Special Warfare Center, Fort Bragg. Kennedy was the main force behind the Special Forces' rapid growth and their extensive deployment in Vietnam.

active VC operating in the south by the end of 1960.

The conflict in the former French colony had been going on for decades, and since the early 1950s the United States had been aiding the government in the southern part of the country with a Military Assistance Advisory Group. South Vietnam's army, the ARVN, seemed incapable of countering the increased incursions by the guerrillas from North Vietnam and by late 1957 the first Special Forces detachments were deployed in an advisory capacity. In December 1960 the National Front for the Liberation of South Vietnam was formed. Composed of the Viet Minh and villagers recruited from the rural areas of South Vietnam itself, this new guerrilla force became known to the world as the Viet Cong. A state of emergency was declared by the Republic's President, Ngo Dinh Diem, and the US increased its commitment. By 1962 the US military presence in Vietnam numbered around 4000 men who, together with the ARVN, were up against an estimated 50,000 VC supported by the NVA, North Vietnam's regular army. The political situation wor-

sened still when Diem was assassinated in November 1963, and leadership of the Republic passed to a succession of short-term leaders. The United States increased its support as the NVA-backed Viet Cong increased their guerrilla activity.

To counter the growth in insurgent activity America devised an Area Development Program. One aspect of this was the Civilian Irregular Defense Group or CIDG. This was established in 1962, and was to become the Special Force's primary commitment to the war in southeast Asia. Concentrated in the Central Highlands of Vietnam the CIDG program covered a region of vital strategic importance. The area, populated by non-Chinese ethnic communities of hill tribesmen, included the border areas of Laos, Cambodia and South Vietnam. Its inhabitants, mainly Montagnards, were discontent with both the old and the new orders, and were ripe for exploitation by the VC.

The CIDG program was initially aimed at converting these tribes to the US/South Vietnamese cause. Special Forces A-Teams, 12-man detachments consisting

BELOW: Special Forces NCOs and their Vietnamese interpreter accompany local forces during operations against the Viet Cong in the Central Plateau region, 1964. The Green Berets were the first American military personnel deployed to Vietnam.

of two officers and 10 non-commissioned specialists, soon won over the hearts and minds of the local population in these remote areas, training the Montagnards and forming them into effective counterinsurgency units. The SF personnel found it easy to develop close working relationships with the tribes, despite the difficulties in communication. In fact only two of them, the Rhade and the Jarai had any form of written language. While the successful CIDG program expanded to cover other areas of South Vietnam and by 1964 constituted a force numbering some 43,000, a special CIDG strike force was being developed under the control of the Special Forces. This gave the local population an offensive rather than a purely defensive capability. By 1964 the CIDG's strike force numbering over 18,000 men, came under the overall command of the 5th Special Forces Group which was to be permanently based in the country. Up until this time the 40 or so CIDG camps had been run by teams from the 1st, 5th and 7th SF Groups. Each team had, until 1964, spent six months with their charges before being replaced. Now a new system was introduced whereby personnel spent a year in place and were then rotated out as individuals rather than teams, thus maintaining a higher degree of continuity.

At the same time as the CIDG program was expanding another SF-sponsored organization was set up to restrict the supply of both weapons and equipment to the VC from across the border. The Special Observation Group, known simply as SOG, was a secret formation formed in 1964 to reduce the flow of VC supplies coming into the country from Laos and Cambodia. SOG remained a closely guarded secret throughout the war, mainly due to the fact that it had to undertake clandestine operations inside both Laos and Cambodia, countries with which the US was not at war. The actual cross-border missions carried out by SOG in these two countries are still classified as secret. SOG teams were composed of 12 men, two SF personnel and 10 Montagnard or Nung tribesmen. Their external missions included sabotage, psychological operations, and subversion. Wearing no recognizable uniform, and carrying nothing to identify themselves, the 'Spike Teams,' as the SOG patrols were codenamed, were normally infiltrated by helicopter. In the event of being engaged by a superior force the Spike Teams could call for an airstrike to cover their exfiltration by helicopter, but were often out of range of artillery support. They were usually very much on their own.

The Special Observation Group was very useful in providing much needed intelligence as to enemy movement, strength and

BELOW: A Green Beret sergeant from the 1st Special Forces Group taking a break during grenade practice with his Vietnamese colleagues at a hilltop outpost. The men are armed with M-14 rifles.

ABOVE: A captain from the 5th Special Forces Group assists a Vietnamese villager in the construction of a new bridge in Chau Doc province. Work like this was undertaken as a part of the revolutionary development program during the late 1960s.

RIGHT: Medical aid was also provided for local Vietnamese villagers as part of the civil-action program. This photograph shows a sergeant 1st class from the 46th Special Forces Company examining a baby at one of the many clinics established by the Green Berets.

ABOVE: A village chief being questioned by members of a Special Forces patrol. With them, wearing tiger-stripe camouflage fatigues and bush hats, are Vietnamese members of the Special Forces Strike Team.

LEFT: A dud bazooka round being cleared from a weapon during contact with Viet Cong guerrillas. Special Forces advisors accompanying Vietnamese patrols were often called on to perform tasks like this.

BELOW: Light equipped but nevertheless armed with an M-16 and a 0.45 pistol, a Special Forces captain checks the perimeter wire of his camp. The Special Forces A-Teams operating in remote areas were under constant threat of NVA or VC attack.

disposition across the borders of the Republic of South Vietnam. The teams undertook countless successful missions and provided the US command with invaluable strategic information regarding the tri-border area.

While the SOG patrols could do little but provide information and harass the enemy, and the CIDG camps were static and often under siege, a new force was formed with the ability to undertake offensive operations against the enemy. In 1965 SF C-Teams were deployed to each of the four corps areas and tasked with raising battalion-sized reaction units. In addition the 7th

Special Forces Group raised a fifth unit capable of providing reinforcements throughout South Vietnam. These new formations were known as Mobile Strike (Mike) Forces.

Each Mike Force had its own attached A-Team, responsible for training, and for providing patrol and platoon leaders. The SF C-Teams were responsible for the organization and command of the Mobile Strike Forces. By the end of 1966 the strength of each Mike Force had increased from one battalion to two or three battalions, and included an integral reconnaissance company and an attached ARVN Special Forces

LEFT: A Special Forces NCO instructing a recruit in the use of the M-79 grenade launcher under the CIDG program. Basic training centers for local civilian recruits were run by the Vietnamese Special Forces (LLBD) aided by the local A-Team.

RIGHT: The paratrooper in the foreground, with spare grenade pins in his helmet band, carries the patrol's radio in addition to smoke grenades for use in marking out landing zones for helicopters.

BELOW: Members of a lightly equipped foot patrol moving through a rice paddy. While crossing such open areas, patrols were in danger of ambush.

team. It was usual for the Vietnamese SF, known as Lac Luong Dac Beit (LLDB), to run the unit's administration while the US A-Teams concentrated on the combat operations. In late 1967 CIDG set up an additional formation, known as the Guerrilla Strike Force, responsible for ambushing and raiding within enemy-controlled areas inside the borders of South Vietnam. The role of the Mike Forces also became more offensive, and they conducted four battalion-sized airborne assaults between 1967 and 1969.

The application of the airborne concept was not generally suited to the war in Vietnam. Indeed the French defeat in Indo-China had culminated in a large-scale – and costly – parachute operation at the siege of Dien Bien Phu. Classic airborne operations, where the deployment of troops by parachute would divide an enemy force and deny it territory, were not really applicable defeating highly mobile guerrillas. The parachute was used fairly extensively in Vietnam, but almost exclusively for Special Forces operations, such as infiltrating SOG teams or dropping Mike Force battalions for reinforcement or relief missions. The use of paratroopers in the same role as they had been employed in World War II or Korea, did not occur in southeast Asia.

The single major parachute deployment of airborne troops occurred toward the latter part of February 1967. The 2nd Battalion of the 503rd Parachute Infantry Regiment, led by Brigadier General John R Deane, jumped into action from the newly introduced C-130 Hercules aircraft to the north of the Tay Ninh city as part of Operation Junction City. The battalion belonged to the 173rd Airborne Brigade which now belonged to the 101st Airborne Division. The latter division had been re-designated as an airmobile formation, and the use of paratroopers in this instance was by way of an experiment. By deploying from fixed-wing aircraft the 2nd Battalion received 60 Huey and six Chinook helicopters for use by the 1st Infantry Division and its divisional artillery.

The operation was a success. The 780 paratroopers jumped from 13 C-130s and their equipment was dropped after them from a further eight aircraft. There were only 11 casualties caused by the drop, most of them slight. The 1st Infantry Division's troops airlanded by helicopter and the operation continued into the middle of May, with the ground troops supported throughout by helicopter. It ended with the US forces in control of an area which had been a VC stronghold from before the defeat of the

French, many years before. The entire operation accounted for 2700 enemy dead, 800 tons of rice captured and destroyed, and large amounts of ammunition and medical supplies seized. However this jump marked the last use of paratroopers in the airborne role during the Vietnam War. If the US and ARVN had invaded North Vietnam there might have been plenty of scope for the airborne deployment of paratroopers, but America adopted a defensive posture and had little need for an airborne 'blocking' force. The new elite units were to be airmobile formations.

Although the US armed forces had made use of helicopters for casualty evacuation during the Korean War and the US Marine Corps had conducted a series of pioneering airmobile assault trials, the Pentagon had not been convinced that the helicopter could be used extensively on the battlefield. However the Howse Board in August 1962 suggested 'the adoption by the army of the airmobile concept,' saying that the large scale use of helicopters was both 'necessary and desirable.'

The 11th Air Assault Division (Test) was formed and tasked with putting theory into practice. The results of the following trials were so successful that the order was given to prepare for active service. The 11th Division was reinforced by men of the 2nd Infantry Division, and the 1st Cavalry Division (Airmobile) came into existence in July 1965. In August the Air Cavalry's lead elements arrived in Vietnam to establish a base which was to become the world's largest helipad. The remainder of the 1st Cavalry Division, 16,000 strong with 400 aircraft and 1600 vehicles, embarked on troopships for Vietnam. On arrival the 1st Air Cav, as the division soon became known, conducted a few small-scale operations against local guerrilla units. After establishing a maintenance and logistical supply base at An Khe, the division began to try out its newly developed tactics for real.

The 1st Cavalry Division had hardly got into its stride before it was flung into a major combat operation, the Battle of the Ia Drang valley. In October 1965 NVA troops attacked the Special Forces camp at Plei Me, about 25 miles from the border with Cambodia. The SF compound was part of the CIDG program, used as a base for training and equipping Montagnard tribesmen. The Montag-

ABOVE: Members of the 173rd Airborne Brigade await the arrival of a helicopter to recover the body of their dead comrade wrapped in a poncho.

ABOVE RIGHT: Under Special Forces supervision members of the CIDG program await their turn to fire the 40mm grenade-launcher at the III Corps basic training center.

RIGHT: Reconnaissance by a small boat. Men of the 5th Special Forces Group patrol a river after a VC mortar attack on their base camp.

LEFT: Special Forces advisors move across open ground with a South Vietnamese patrol. As their personal weapons are carried slung over their shoulders rather than held at the ready it is unlikely that they are in an operational area.

ABOVE: This shoulder insignia was worn by members of the 1st Air Cavalry's Air Assault teams which operated in Vietnam.

nards and their advisers beat back the enemy but the intensity of the attack and the size of the unit involved meant further attacks were most likely. The attacking force, the NVA's 33rd Infantry Regiment suffered heavily at Plei Me. It lost almost 900 men killed and 100 men missing, while a further 500 had been wounded.

Despite the heavy casualties the 33rd Regiment had not been destroyed and had pulled back into the Ia Drang valley, still inside South Vietnam, where it regrouped and was joined by the 32nd and later the 66th NVA Infantry Regiments. The task of destroying the enemy was given to the 1st Air Cav's 3rd Brigade, known as the Garry Owen Brigade, which comprised the 1st and 2nd Battalions of the 7th Cavalry. Joined for the operation by a third battalion, the three units moved into the Ia Drang to conduct a two-day 'search and destroy' mission under the command of Colonel Thomas W Brown. The initial plan had called for 24 supporting helicopters. In the event only 16 aircraft were available for the brigade's operation, and in addition only two 105mm howitzers were provided for artillery cover.

The brigade command post was set up and Colonel Brown, together with Lieutenant Colonel Harold Moore of the 1st Battalion, planned for the operation to begin at first light. One problem that the two officers had to contend with was a manpower shortage. Troops rotating out of the country at the end of their tours had not been replaced quickly enough, and a number of men were sick with malaria and other diseases. The 1st Battalion was reduced to two-thirds of its established strength.

The plan entailed the maximum use of helicopters, requiring large landing zones (LZs) capable of taking at least 10 helicopters each. There were only three LZs in the area. The stepping off point was to be Plei Me and preliminary reconnaissance of the tentative LZs showed one to be completely unsuitable. An additional flight down the Ia Drang valley from Plei Me suggested that the second LZ was also unsuitable, while the third had signs of the enemy on a nearby trail. In the event the latter LZ was chosen for the initial assault.

Colonel Moore was aware that helicopter flights over the area had undoubtedly

ABOVE: A patrol of the 1st Cavalry Division (Airmobile) interrogating Vietnamese farmers through an interpreter. Local villagers were able to provide information about VC and NVA activities on a number of occasions.

warned the enemy and ordered diversionary fire to be put down on the two rejected LZs. Company B was the first into the area, followed by Companies A, C and D. Four platoons, each comprising four UH-1D Hueys, moved into the area, and landed after the ground had been prepared by fire from gunships. Company B landed successfully and moved off the LZ, followed by Companies A and C. The NVA began to fight back, and by the time the fifth airlift arrived the LZ was under smallarms fire. The fight that ensued was a fierce and bloody one, heralding a battle that continued for the next two days. Forward units of the Air Cav engaged enemy units, trying to pin them down, or advanced toward suspected enemy positions with the aim of drawing fire and locating the NVA. The North Vietnamese realized that they were being destroyed by artillery or ground-attack aircraft once they had been located, so moved in close to the American ground positions. Some of these positions were overrun by sheer weight of numbers, and many of the actions ended in fierce hand-to-hand combat. One dead platoon commander was located with five

enemy dead in and around his foxhole, while another dead trooper had to have his fingers prised away from the throat of an NVA soldier.

The 1st Air Cav had proved its ability to land the maximum number of troops in the shortest time into the smallest area during the Ia Drang battle. In addition it could drop units at different LZs and by doing so encircle the enemy. The 1st Air Cav's determined attack on the NVA forces in the Ia Drang paid off handsomely. By mid-November the first major NVA offensive inside South Vietnam had lost its momentum and they had lost an estimated 1800 men. The 1st Air Cav's casualties during the initial stages of the operation had been relatively light, 79 men killed and 121 wounded. Their aircraft had stood up well, with only four shot down out of the total of 59 that had taken hits. The 1st Cavalry Division (Airmobile) continued to serve in Vietnam for the remainder of America's involvement, taking part in a number of operations including the US offensive into Cambodia. But Ia Drang was its first major engagement, the testing ground of a new elite. The helicopter and the airmobility concept had been proven in combat.

The support of the South Vietnamese government by the United States required a massive input of material as well as manpower. As the various American services, army, air force, Marines and navy, became increasingly involved in the conflict, the need to supply the South's armed forces became even more vital. The South Vietnamese required vast quantities of weapons, equipment and other war supplies, almost all of which had to be transported by sea. Control of the sea was vital to the American war effort and the US Navy provided the protection needed by Allied shipping.

In addition to its role in the protection afforded the maritime movement of equipment and other supplies, and its carrier-launched bombing war against North Vietnam, the US Navy conducted combat operations in the many waterways snaking throughout Vietnam. Hundreds of large and small logistics craft provided the vital supply link between the maritime fleet and land bases often far inland. With control of the seas the US Navy was capable of projecting its strength along the inland waterways and, within areas such as the Mekong Delta, conducting a campaign against the VC.

The low-lying Mekong Delta, together with the nearby forests and rice-growing areas of the Ca Mau Peninsula, comprises

around one quarter of South Vietnam, and favored VC guerrilla operations. The waterways, consisting of rivers criss-crossed with a web of canals, were to prove the battleground for the navy's unconventional 'brown water' fleet. Riverine warfare of this nature caused a number of special units to be formed. These formations were primarily engaged in conducting their own or assisting their Vietnamese counterparts in a variety of combat and support tasks. They consisted of the River Patrol Force, the Mobile Riverine Force, the Coastal Surveillance Force and the Naval Advisory Group. In 1968 the introduction of NVA forces into the inland waterways led to the increase in offensive riverine operations.

The River Patrol Force was established in 1966 to sever enemy supply routes, and to conduct search and destroy missions against troop concentrations and supply bases. The force was equipped with Patrol Boats, River, (PBRs) and UH-1B helicopters. The 31-foot craft were armed with three .5-inch machine guns, an M-60 machine gun and a 40mm grenade-launcher. They had a top speed of 25 knots, provided by a water jet propulsion system, were extremely maneuverable, and had an 18-inch draft. Operating in conjunction with the helicopters, codenamed 'Seawolves' the PBRs carried out an effective campaign against the waterborne VC and NVA.

ABOVE: Mobile Riverine Force monitor laying down fire with a flame-thrower during one of the many patrols along the tributaries of the Mekong. Possible ambush positions were often reconnoitered by fire in an effort to draw out the enemy.

LEFT: A turret-mounted, twin 0.5 caliber heavy machine gun clearly demonstrates the superior firepower of the navy's riverine forces.

RIGHT: A strike assault boat (STAB) on a high-speed patrol near the Cambodian border. These small craft relied on speed to get them out of trouble.

Another asset in the American armory was the Mobile Riverine Force (MRF). A joint army-navy assault force, the MRF combined combat units from the 9th Infantry Division with assault craft and crews of the River Assault Flotilla No 1. Its primary mission was to deploy rapid-reaction forces against enemy troop concentrations, and the MRF operated on a larger scale than the River Patrol Force. Equipped with amphibious armored troop carriers (ATCs), capable of carrying 40 troops and providing close support, the MRF could operate in virtually any waterway with a depth of five feet and width enough to turn the craft around. In addition to the ATCs the Riverine Force had three types of boats specially designed to protect the infantry element and provide support for them once they had landed. The foremost of these vessels were the monitors which, like the ATCs themselves, were converted landing craft (LCM-6s). They were armed with a variety of heavy machine guns, automatic grenade-launchers, an 81mm mortar and either a 40mm cannon or a 105mm howitzer mounted in a forward turret. The monitors were capable of putting down a devastating field of fire. The second type of craft operated by the MRF was a Command and Communications Boat (CCB), similar to the monitor but with less weaponry and more communications equipment. The CCBs provided a vital link between the army's battalion commanders and the navy's river squadron commanders, and a base from which operations and movement could be directed.

Unlike the ATCs, monitors and CCBs, the Mobile Riverine Force operated one type of river boat which had been purpose-built – the Assault Support Patrol Boat (ASPB). Unlike the other vessels which were converted or adapted for use by the MRF employing the LCM-6 hull, the ASPB was specially designed and constructed to fill the naval riverine force's requirement for a fast escort and patrol boat. With a top speed of 15 knots (as opposed to the eight knots of the assault craft) the ASPB greatly expanded the range of the MRF's interdiction patrols.

In addition to the surface assault and patrol vessels the MRF employed 'mini-aircraft carriers.' Four ATCs were modified by the addition of a helipad constructed above the forward deck capable of accommodating a UH-1 Huey, and a fifth craft, designated as a 'refueling platform,' also had a helipad. These vessels proved a great asset to the MRF, especially when immediate resupply or casualty evacuation missions were required by friendly forces.

TOP LEFT: A heavily armed monitor leading a river patrol along a Mekong Delta canal.

CENTER LEFT: A squadron base in the Mekong Delta. A number of small craft are tied up alongside their mother ship lying off in mid-stream.

BELOW LEFT: Amphibious armored troop carriers (ATCs) of the MRF move up close to the shore in a search for North Vietnamese forces in the Delta area.

ABOVE: An infantry patrol aboard an assault support patrol boat (ASPB). Unlike other MRF vessels, these craft were specially constructed for riverine operations.

After initial operations in the Rung Sat Special Zone the Mobile Riverine Force moved into the Mekong Delta. In late May 1967 a force comprising five ships set up a Mobile Riverine base. This force included two self-propelled barracks ships, the USS *Benewah* and the USS *Colleton*; a landing-craft repair ship, the USS *Askari*; the barracks craft *APL-6*; and a logistical support ship provided on a two-month rotational basis by the US Seventh Fleet. Together, these five vessels provided repair and logistical support which included accommodation, messing and working space for the 1900 men of the army's 2nd Brigade and the 1600 naval personnel belonging to Task Force 117. By mid-June the force had 68 river craft, a complement that grew larger month by month until a total figure of 180 river assault boats was reached in 1968.

From the beginning the MRF conducted six to eight search and destroy missions per month, each patrol lasting between two or three days. A number of these patrols were carried out in conjunction with the South Vietnamese Navy and proved to be very successful. It was estimated that in each of the eight missions conducted in mid to late 1967 enemy casualties averaged 100 killed. The largest single engagement occurred in

December, when the MRF and the 5th Battalion of the South Vietnamese Marine Corps attacked and overran elements of the 502nd VC Local Force and the 267th NVA Battalion.

During a routine patrol up the Rach Ruong canal some 40 MRF assault craft were engaged and hit by intense fire from automatic weapons, recoilless rifles and rockets. Over a score received substantial damage. Despite this, and having taken a number of casualties, a landing was carried out and the Vietnamese Marines, supported by fire from the assault craft, attacked and captured a series of fortified bunkers. The quick, daring and determined assault overwhelmed the NVA defenders. Enemy dead included 266 bodies found on the battlefield. In addition 126 sampans were sunk and 161 bunkers destroyed. Allied casualties were light: the Vietnamese lost 41 Marines dead; the MRF only 11. None of the US Navy vessels involved in the two-day operation was sunk.

The MRF was also heavily involved in countering the costly Tet Offensive launched by the VC throughout South Vietnam in late January 1968. The offensive, which coincided with the Vietnamese public holiday, was particularly vicious.

Civilian casualties were high, with the VC opening fire upon fleeing refugees indiscriminately. Government officials, their families, and off-duty military personnel caught up in the surprise attack were all butchered, often in the most brutal fashion. The Delta area was particularly hard hit.

Throughout the offensive, which lasted over a week, the men of the MRF used all available craft to move the entire force from one area of fighting to another. Continuous operations were conducted during the period of the offensive and when it was over the MRF had accounted for over 650 enemy dead, the capture of a number of weapons caches, and tons of ammunition and other supplies seized. The most important aspect of the MRF's activity had been its ability to move rapidly and deploy large bodies of troops where most needed. The 'brown water navy' succeeded in preventing the VC from achieving a single important victory in the Delta, a fact that did not go unnoticed by General Westmoreland who later remarked that the MRF had 'saved the Delta.'

The US Navy's riverine forces continued to deny the VC the use of the inland waterways and canal systems of South Vietnam. Government order was re-established in the Mekong Delta, an area which had harbored tens of thousands of Viet Cong, and an area which contained one-third of South Vietnam's total population and had been the scene of 30-odd years of continuous guerrilla warfare. The Mobile Riverine Force and River Patrol Force constituted a highly specialized and unusual elite, and demonstrated the flexibility of the world's most powerful navy in tackling the world's most successful guerrillas.

The United States Navy had two further specialist units which operated in southeast Asia during the Vietnam War. These consisted of the Underwater Demolition Teams (UDTs) and the SEAL (Sea Air & Land) Teams. The primary mission of the UDTs was one of beach reconnaissance and clearance. UDT combat swimmers were responsible for clearing or identifying all obstacles from the six-and-a-half fathom curve (depth 21 feet) to the highwater mark in advance of

ABOVE: A member of UDT 12 prepares to exit from a C-47 transport for a free-fall descent near the naval amphibious base, Coronado, California.

ABOVE LEFT: UDT swimmers, wearing wet-suits and fins, undergoing parachute training.

The total Combat Demolition Unit team losses during the difficult assault averaged 41 percent.

Those personnel who survived Normandy were shipped back to the United States. Lessons were learned, and new techniques were tried out during a six-week training program in Hawaii. The structure of the CDU was also changed and the teams went from six-man units to groups of two or three men. Several of these groups were formed into a squadron and became Underwater Demolition Teams. Most UDT missions were conducted in the Pacific and UDTs were involved in operations against the Japanese in Borneo, Peleliu, Saipan, Guam, Iwo Jima and Okinawa. The new training and tactics, together with the revised structure, paid off and the casualty rate fell to one percent. At the end of World War II there were 34 active UDTs and the organization incorporated some 3500 personnel. In 1946 29 UDTs were demobilized. Two UDTs were assigned to the Atlantic Fleet and the remaining three deployed to the Pacific.

In 1950 the UDTs were again in action. They took part in the amphibious landings at Inchon, and carried out a number of sabotage missions against North Korean targets such as bridges and railroad tracks. The UDTs continued to conduct routine tasks such as channel clearance and beach reconnaissance until the end of the Korean War in 1953. The Vietnam War gave the UDTs yet another chance to demonstrate their skills. One complete team was deployed to the Philippines from where it dispatched various units to operational areas in southeast Asia. Detachment Alpha provided training and support to the operational units. Detachment Bravo supplied Beach Reconnaissance Groups while Detachment Charlie conducted combat recon missions from the USS *Perch* and the USS *Tunney*, two fleet class submarines.

Detachment Charlie perfected two methods of deployment from the subs. One involved exiting the submarine while it was submerged; the second method consisted of floating off the deck of a diving submarine. Both 'wet' and 'dry' methods were successful and their use depended on operational requirements. Detachment Delta was based at Danang from where it conducted a wide range of sabotage missions. Detachments Echo and Foxtrot were assigned to the Amphibious Ready Group and conducted recon and demolition tasks, while Detachments Golf and Hotel operated with the riverine forces. These latter two detachments worked mainly with the River Patrol Force (RPF), operating from their

ABOVE: SEALs working for Task Force 116 prepare to depart from a river patrol boat base at Binh Thuy for a night operation.

amphibious landings. Any obstacle, manmade or otherwise, that could prevent the movement of landing craft or supply vessels, was destroyed by the UDTs with explosives. In addition to these activities UDT personnel were responsible for marking out safe channels, guiding in the first amphibious wave, and obtaining intelligence for the amphibious task force commander. Secondary tasks included the infiltration and exfiltration of agents or Special Forces teams, and the sabotage of enemy shipping or harbors.

The navy's Underwater Demolition Teams started with the formation of the first Combat Demolition Unit in mid-1943 at Fort Pierce, Florida. Volunteers for this special force came from navy Construction Battalions (CBs) and navy or Marine Corps scout and raider units. After undergoing intensive training the men were divided into six-man teams and sent to England prior to the Allied invasion of Normandy. Before and during D-Day these teams carried out their assigned missions, but their casualties were high. Some teams were wiped out to a man.

ABOVE: Armed with a variety of weapons, including the Stoner machine gun used exclusively by the SEALs, part of the detachment attached to Task Force 116 awaits inspection by the Secretary of the Navy.

LEFT: Two members of a SEAL team and their Vietnamese ally (foreground) aboard a patrol craft on their way to an operation.

ABOVE RIGHT: The 9th Marine Expeditionary Brigade comes ashore at Danang. The vehicle in the center of the picture is a mechanical mule.

RIGHT: Members of a SEAL team prepare to come ashore.

PBRs which were crewed by sailors of the Special Boat Squadrons. Together the men of Golf, Hotel and the RPF carried out missions in the Mekong Delta area, and often engaged the VC and NVA up to 100 miles from the sea.

While the UDTs operated in, on or under the water, the second naval special warfare unit spent most of its time conducting operations ashore. The US Navy's SEAL teams originated from a study conducted in 1960 which analyzed the navy's ability to carry out counterinsurgency operations, including covert and unconventional warfare. The commander of navy operations realized the need for the US Navy to have its own special forces unit and in 1962 President Kennedy commissioned SEAL Teams 1 and 2. These new formations became part of Naval Special Warfare Groups which comprised the two SEAL teams, the UDTs, and the Special Boat squadrons. The SEAL teams became part of the fleet's tactical units. Their personnel received the same initial training as the UDTs but went on to learn the skills required to conduct limited counterinsurgency operations. These skills included medical aid, civil engineering, small boat operation and maintenance, and basic education theory. They were being used in training the South Vietnamese civilian population and militia in local defense, in the same way as the army's Green Berets ran the CIDG program.

With the increased US involvement as the Vietnam War escalated SEAL Teams 1 and 2 deployed platoon-sized groups into the riverine areas. These small groups were usually inserted and extracted by fast river craft. As operations increased the SEALs were equipped with the quieter ASPBs, which increased their range while giving them greater firepower if ambushed while traveling to or from an operation. In late 1966 the SEAL teams received a special support 'package' comprising a UH-1B 'Seawolf' helicopter, a Boat Support Unit and a Mobile Support Team. This increased support proved of immense value to the SEAL platoons which were often greatly outnumbered by the enemy they were fighting and needed a reliable and rapid back-up.

The SEAL teams, like their UDT and Special Boat squadron colleagues, continued to operate throughout America's involvement in the war. The number of missions began to decrease with the gradual US withdrawal but in late 1970 the SEALs were responsible for a highly successful and much acclaimed attack on a VC prisoner of war camp. In a combined operation, a 15-man SEAL platoon together with a 19-man militia unit, carried out a daring assault on the camp, releasing a number of South Vietnamese captives, some of whom had been prisoner for over four years. This was just one operation of many carried out during 1970 and the SEALs were ultimately responsible for recovering a total of 46 POWs from VC captivity.

During their time in Vietnam the SEAL teams accounted for more than 800 VC killed during contacts, and an even larger number captured. For their continuous skill and professionalism the SEALs received two Presidential Unit Citations, and personal awards included one Medal of Honor, two Navy Crosses and 402 Silver Stars.

Although the United States Marine Corps had no special operations forces such as the army's Green Berets or the navy's SEALs, it is nevertheless a superior military formation. The concept of an 'elite within an elite' had essentially ended during the latter stages of World War II with the demise of the raider battalions. The Corps was however seriously involved in the war in Vietnam where, for the most part, it was deployed in the ground infantry role.

The Marines' initial involvement in the conflict began in 1962 when 24 UH-34D heli-

TOP LEFT: Marines wait for a C-123 transport.

ABOVE LEFT: Marine infantry take shelter in Hue.

ABOVE: Marines patrolling after the Tet Offensive.

TOP: Supported by an M-60 tank, Marines conduct a search.

TOP RIGHT: The siege at Khe Sanh.

LEFT: The aftermath of a rocket attack at Khe Sanh. Marines clear the blazing debris.

copters were deployed to Soc Trang, the area to the southwest of Saigon in support of the South Vietnamese armed forces. In early 1965 Marine Corps antiaircraft detachments were sent to South Vietnam to support the air strikes being conducted against the North, but it was not until later in 1965 that the USMC became heavily involved. In March the Marines were ordered ashore and established bases in and around Danang, with the aim of eventually controlling the five northernmost provinces of South Vietnam. As the conflict escalated so the Marines' involvement increased. Operating immediately south of the De-Militarized Zone (DMZ), which divided the north and south of Vietnam, the USMC bore the brunt of much of the war's heaviest fighting, not only on the ground but in the air as well. The

Marines' combined amphibious, ground, and air assets were invaluable to the army's commander, General Westmoreland. In 1968 they were responsible for the recapture of a number of towns and cities taken by the VC and NVA during the Tet Offensive, notably Hue, and were also responsible for the successful defense of the base at Khe Sanh, which was besieged by a strong NVA force dedicated to overcoming its American defenders.

In 1968 the Marines comprised 24 of the 52 infantry battalions that made up I Corps. This corps also included such units as the 101st Airborne Division and the 1st Cavalry Division (Airmobile). The Marine Corps was providing almost half of I Corps' ground troops and much of its air support.

During the gradual withdrawal of US troops from early 1969 onward, Marine units supported ARVN forces replacing the outgoing American battalions. By September 1970 only three Regiments of the 1st Marine Division remained in Vietnam. The 5th and 7th Marines departed and the III Marine Amphibious Force (MAF) was replaced by the 3rd Marine Amphibious Brigade (MAB). The US military presence in Vietnam diminished and by July 1971 the only Marines left were the Embassy guards, with some advisers and technicians. The communist Easter Offensive in 1972 heralded the departure of all US troops. Marine aviation units were called in to cover the withdrawal but no Marines were involved in the fighting on the ground. The Marines' war in southeast Asia left 12,936 men dead and 88,594 wounded. It proved a costly conflict but one in which the USMC played a major role.

AFTER the evacuation of the US Embassy staff from Saigon in 1975 US air bases in Thailand assumed greater strategic importance. So too did the Gulf of Thailand, especially the area off the Cambodian coast through which US shipping sailed. It was off this coastline, controlled by the Khmer Rouge, that an incident occurred that led to the involvement of a group of hand-picked Marines in an ambitious rescue operation.

On 12 May 1975 the American registered cargo freighter, SS *Mayaguez*, was seized by Cambodian gunboats approximately six-and-a-half miles off Poulo Wai. Before radio communications ceased the ship's captain managed to send a signal informing the outside world he was being boarded by the Khmer Rouge. Within hours Washington had been informed, and five-and-a-half hours after the seizure the US National

planned US Navy A-7 Corsair IIs and F-4 Phantoms kept Cambodian craft away from the captured vessel. 'Enemy' shipping attempting to enter the area was engaged and at least three vessels were sunk. While diplomatic efforts were being applied to secure the release of the crew two Marine companies were flown from Okinawa to the base at U-Tapao, bringing the total number of available personnel to around 600. At the time several US warships were steaming toward the area at full speed.

By the evening of the 14th it became clear that diplomacy was useless and the rescue operation was given the go-ahead. What was not clear at this time was the location of the hostage crew. Intelligence reports suggested that they may have been taken off the vessel by fishing boat and imprisoned on the island of Koh Tang.

CHAPTER 4

PEACEKEEPING FORCES

Security Council held a meeting to discuss the incident. As a result of this meeting close aerial observation of the stricken vessel was ordered while plans were drawn up for the rescue of the ship's 39 captured crew members.

Monitored by a navy P-3C Orion patrol plane the *Mayaguez* remained at anchor off Poulo Wai, while AC-130 Spectre gunships of USAF Special Operations were instructed to disable the *Mayaguez* should the Cambodians attempt to move it. Meanwhile a rescue force, consisting of eight HH-53 helicopters of the 3rd Aerospace Rescue and Recovery Squadron, together with eight CH-53 aircraft from the 21st Special Operations Squadron, was tasked with transporting 75 USAF security police to a position from where they could mount an assault. On the move one of the aircraft went down with the loss of all five crew members and the 18 passengers.

As the rescue operation was being

At first light on the morning of 15 May a formation of eight CH-53 and three HH-53 helicopters landed the first Marine assault force on the two northern beaches of Koh Tang, codenamed West and East. One of the two CH-53s was hit after dropping off its load of Marines on West Beach and made it 1000 yards offshore before ditching. The second CH-53, together with a third and an HH-53 from the second assault wave, approached the beach, dropped their Marines and flew out back over the sea. Engaged by smallarms fire, missiles and mortars, all three aircraft took a number of hits.

The helicopter landings on East Beach experienced similar difficulties. Ground fire took out one helicopter which crashed in the surf, forcing the 21 Marines and the air force crew to battle their way ashore. A second aircraft burst into flames on impact with the water, killing eight men outright. A further four were hit and killed while swimming out to sea. The 14 survivors were later

LEFT: US Marines boarding the merchant ship SS *Mayaguez* after the operation to secure the release of the crew.

BELOW LEFT: Crew of the *Mayaguez* take a rest after managing to evade their Khmer Rouge captors during the Marine assaults on East and West beaches.

BELOW: Crossdecking from the USS *Harold E Holt*, Marines board the *Mayaguez* to look around.

picked up by a US destroyer, although one later died of his wounds. Within an hour of the first wave landing 14 men had been killed or were missing, three helicopters were down, and two more were severely damaged. In addition a total of 54 Marines and aircrew were pinned down by enemy fire on the beaches.

While the fighting raged on the beaches a boarding party from the USS *Holt* found the *Mayaguez* abandoned and took it in tow. The operation began to take shape. Meanwhile the crew of the *Mayaguez*, together with the crew of a captured Thai fishing vessel, managed to evade their Khmer Rouge captors. In the confusion created by the Marine assaults on East and West Beaches, the crews managed to escape to the Thais' boat and put to sea. Within an hour they were picked up by a US destroyer.

Fierce fighting continued on the beaches. On East Beach a second landing was made but unfortunately the Marines were dropped some way from the main body, and had to spend several hours fighting to reach it. Now that the crew of *Mayaguez* had been recovered, the way was clear for the use of aggressive air support. An AC-130 Spectre gunship provided effective fire support for the Marines still pinned down on the beaches, but helicopter resupply and evacuation missions ended with the aircraft taking hits and turning back.

By midday there were 197 men stranded on West Beach and a further 25 stuck on East Beach. A mission to retrieve the beleaguered force was only partially successful and it was not until a USAF C-130 dropped a massive 15,000lb bomb on the center of the island that the recovery of the seriously injured could be effected. Despite this accomplishment, when dusk arrived there were still 202 Marines ashore. A further three helicopters made it to the beaches and managed to pick up 132 men. Under cover of strafing runs by USAF OV-10A Broncos and navy A-7 Corsairs, the remaining Marines withdrew into a tight defensive perimeter a short way from the landing zone. Then as a Spectre gunship poured fire into the Khmer Rouge positions in the treeline above the beach, two helicopters dashed in and lifted out the remaining Marines. With the last two Marines providing cover as they were hauled aboard the helicopters, US troops withdrew from southeast Asia for the last time.

The spectacular, hard-fought and ultimately successful rescue attempt at Koh Tang was over. In total around 230 men had been landed on the two beaches. In all 15 men, Marines and aircrew, had been killed; 49 were wounded and three were missing. Out of the 15 helicopters involved in the rescue operation, four were lost and a further nine were damaged. The cost in terms of manpower and material had been heavy, but not exorbitant. The *Mayaguez* and its crew had been recovered and the hastily mounted operation had achieved its aim. Additionally the US Marine Corps had proved itself capable of mounting such an operation, showing what could be done when specialist units of the various services cooperated.

On 14 November 1979 a group of Iranian 'students' stormed past the Marine Corps guards and took possession of the US Embassy in Teheran, the capital of Iran. In taking over the embassy these armed 'students' also took hostage 53 staff, who were in the building. A further three American nationals were held in the Foreign Ministry. The situation was serious.

A diplomatic solution to the problem was complicated by the anti-American nature of Iran's post-revolutionary regime. The Iranian government professed to have no control over the 'student' captors who held the complex, which itself was surrounded by pro-government 'revolutionary guards' and members of the 'people's militia.' Previous hostage situations had seldom been this complicated. Diplomatic measures

were put into effect with little positive result. President Jimmy Carter became increasingly concerned about the safety of the hostages, and a military option began to be considered in earnest. Planners swung into action.

The chosen plan centered around a recently formed special operations force known as 'Delta,' commanded by Colonel Charles Beckwith. Beckwith had served an attachment with Britain's 22nd Special Air Service Regiment and was a veteran of Special Forces operations in southeast Asia. An uniquely experienced SF officer, Beckwith had convinced the military of the need for a special operations unit formed along similar lines to the SAS. This unit, known as Delta, was formed in April 1979 and began training for unconventional warfare which included counterterrorist operations and hostage rescue.

The rescue operation, with the overall codename 'Eagle Claw,' was particularly complex and involved numerous services and agencies. Time was of the essence, great distances were involved and intelligence sources were varied. The plan proposed by Beckwith was essentially divided into several operational phases.

The initial part of the plan called for Delta to fly by USAF C-141 Starlifters from the US to Masirah airfield, via West Germany and Egypt. At the former RAF airfield on the island of Masirah, off the coast of Oman, Delta force would transfer to three USAF Special Operations Wing MC-130 aircraft and fly direct to a rendezvous, codenamed Desert One, inside Iran. Desert One was a remote site in the Dasht-e-Karir salt desert, approximately 300 miles southeast of Tehran. Meanwhile eight navy RH-53D helicopters, flown by Marine Corps crews, would take off from the USS *Nimitz* and arrive at Desert One 30 minutes after the main party. The plan called for both aircraft types to fly in at very low level to avoid being picked up by Iranian radar. The helicopter element of the operation was codenamed 'Evening Light.' The aircraft themselves were specially chosen. The RH-53D helicopter is a naval version of the HH-53 'Jolly Green Giant.' Aside from being less obvious than military troop transport helicopters, the main reason for the choice of the RH-53Ds was their improved payload and performance. The choice of these aircraft was to play a decisive part in the operation's failure.

The rescue operation as planned was divided into three phases. The insertion,

BELOW: Aircrew inspecting their RH-53D helicopter on the flight-deck of the USS *Nimitz*.

phase one; the rescue, phase two; and the extraction, phase three. The rescue force, comprising Delta, Rangers and a Special Forces A Team, would rendezvous at Desert One for the first phase of the operation. Delta's three MC-130s would be joined by eight RH-53s from the USS *Nimitz*, and three EC-130 command and control aircraft. The C-130s would carry extra fuel for the eight helicopters. The helicopters were the vital link. An absolute minimum of six machines was needed to successfully complete the mission.

On landing the first priority was to deploy a road-watch team to control the road next to the landing strip, intercepting and detaining any local traffic. The rescue teams would then fly out in the refueled helicopters to a forward landing zone where they would be met by intelligence agents who would provide transport to the Embassy and Foreign Ministry. The helicopters would then fly to a remote wadi nearby, where they would lie up in a concealed hide position until the Embassy assault group went in. Once at the Embassy Delta would divide into three groups and assault the complex from different directions, while the Special Forces A Team released the hostages from the Foreign Ministry. Delta would then secure a landing zone

for the evacuation of the hostages. Meanwhile a Ranger company would attack and secure an airfield at Manzariyeh, some 35 miles to the south of Teheran. This airfield would then be used as a staging point for the released hostages. The helicopters would pick up the hostages and their rescuers from either the Embassy compound or a nearby sports stadium, fly them to Manzariyeh, where they would transfer to USAF C-141 Starlifters for the final extraction phase.

Initially the operation went according to plan. The C-141 Starlifters transferred Delta at Masirah airfield, and the first C-130 flew into the strip at Desert One without incident. The road-watch team, consisting of both Delta and Ranger personnel, deployed and immediately detained a busload of Iranians. Two more vehicles appeared shortly after the bus had been stopped. The first, a tanker, was engaged by a light anti-tank weapon and exploded. The second vehicle escaped. The remaining C-130s flew into Desert One with the rest of the force and the fuel for the helicopters. A total of four aircraft then remained while two returned to Masirah. Then the long wait for the arrival of the helicopters began.

The RH-53s began to experience difficulties shortly after making landfall at the end of the 50-mile flight across the sea from the USS *Nimitz*. The instruments aboard helicopter No 6 indicated impending rotor blade failure and the aircraft had to abort, its crew being recovered by helicopter No 8 which was following along behind. Then an hour later the seven-ship flight ran into a severe dust storm, a meteorological phenomenon known locally as an 'haboob.' Helicopters No 1 and No 2 were forced down, but after a brief period on the ground, these two aircraft, one of which had lost its inertial navigation system, took off and headed for Desert One. Meanwhile helicopter No 5 was experiencing problems with its gyro, tactical navigation system and radar. With vital instruments down and mountains in front this aircraft had no option but to abort. Only six helicopters now remained, the absolute minimum needed to carry out the operation within the safety parameters laid down in the final plan.

With helicopter No 3 leading, the strung-out formation eventually made it to Desert One and proceeded to refuel. The operation was already 90 minutes behind schedule when the assault teams began to board their assigned aircraft. As this was being effected an already frustrated Beckwith was informed that helicopter No 2 had suffered irreparable hydraulics failure. Now down to five helicopters the mission had to be aborted. This itself presented no real problem despite the fact that the rescue force had not practised abort procedures during its training. The only complication was the fuel status of helicopter No 4. Rather than shut down the aircraft on landing the crew had kept the engines running and helicopter No 4, having used more fuel than the others, needed to tank up. Only one C-130 had enough fuel remaining and to give the aircraft room to refuel helicopter No 3 had to move out of the way. On taking off helicopter No 3 banked to the left but had difficulty gaining lift. This was mainly due to Desert One's height above sea-level (5000 feet) coupled with the helicopter's gross weight (42,000lbs).

Unable to maintain a hover the pilot banked his aircraft to the right and, in the darkness collided with the tanker aircraft. The result was both instantaneous and disasterously impressive. Both aircraft exploded. Five USAF crew in the C-130 were killed as were three Marine aircrew aboard the RH-53. However with the aircraft on fire and ammunition detonating around them, 64 Delta personnel in the fuel-laden rear of the C-130 managed to escape from the stricken plane, taking their loadmaster with them. Beckwith, having already ordered the

abort now had to give the order for the helicopters to be abandoned. The rescue force loaded up the three remaining C-130s and flew back to Masirah. The rescue mission had failed.

Post-mission analysis into the reasons for the failure of Operation Eagle Claw continued for months afterwards. Without doubt the mission had been plagued by a series of misfortunes but the blame could not be laid with the troops on the ground.

America's allies came up with numerous suggestions. Britain, which had two SAS observers with Delta during the planning stage of the operation, maintained that the helicopters were unsuited to their task and that there were too few of them. Most interested parties generally agreed that 10 would have been the minimum number. The Israelis, with experience in mounting this type of operation, insisted that such missions required a 100 percent safety margin, and that a total of 16 helicopters should have been deployed from the *Nimitz*. Whatever the various reasons for the operation's failure to move on from Desert One, the fact remains that the prevailing weather conditions and the likely performance of the aircraft should have been realized before the outset of the operation. However, much can be learned in hindsight and America's next hostage release mission had a markedly different outcome.

RIGHT: A jeep patrol of the 24th Marine Amphibious Unit (MAU) moves through downtown Beirut. The Marine Corps suffered heavy casualties during their peacekeeping operations in the Lebanon.

BELOW: Members of the 82nd Airborne Division assemble pictured after disembarking from a C-5 transport aircraft at the beginning of an RDF overseas deployment.

In the years that followed America's involvement in the war in southeast Asia, the US military attempted to maintain a low profile in international affairs, although US troops continued to play an important role in peacekeeping operations and were active with UN forces in the Sinai and Beirut. The US government's two recent attempts to secure the release of American hostages had met with limited success, but public opinion toward the military was changing. The vehement antimilitary feeling that had surfaced in the United States in the later part of the Vietnam War had declined to be replaced by casual disinterest. The regular army had ended conscription and the failure of the Iranian rescue mission had led to the critical re-evaluation of the requirements for special operations forces and other elite military formations.

The immediate post-Vietnam purges that had been directed against unconventional and unorthodox units had ended. The US Army Special Forces, after a series of serious reductions in terms of battalions, budget and manpower, began to increase in strength. The Marine Corps, after battling in the jungles of Asia as basic infantry, re-affirmed its commitment to the more specialized amphibious role. The US Army's Rangers, dissolved toward the end of World War II, used only intermittently as divisional reconnaissance and regimental reserve troops during the wars in Korea and Vietnam, were officially reinstated as a two-battalion formation with its own individual identity. The Navy's SEALs, always low profile, had been reduced during the post-Vietnam period but continued to exist, as did the UDTs. The 82nd Airborne Division was still intact together with its supporting arms and services, and the 101st Airmobile Division became the specialists in heliborne operations, taking on the role from the 1st Cavalry Division (Airmobile), while at the same time maintaining a limited parachute capability. With these assets the US government and its military leaders were more than capable of mounting an out-of-area operation to rescue American hostages outside the United States.

In October 1983 US President Ronald Reagan received a request from the six-member committee for the Organization of Eastern Caribbean States to restore order on the West Indies' island of Grenada. Follow-

ABOVE LEFT: A Marine sandbagged position in Beirut. These defenses were to prove inadequate against suicide attacks.

ABOVE: Rangers move forward from the drop zone during the invasion of Grenada.

LEFT: Units of the 82nd Airborne Division form up at Point Salines, Grenada.

BELOW LEFT: Parachutes fitted, members of the 82nd Airborne Division board a C-130 transport aircraft.

ABOVE RIGHT: US Navy SEALs being deployed into the water from a fast-moving patrol boat.

FAR RIGHT: A seven-man SEAL patrol display their weapons and equipment during an exercise.

RIGHT: US Navy SEALs at work under water. Their training is both demanding and dangerous.

ing the assassination of the island's leader, Maurice Bishop, together with members of his cabinet and the murders of a number of labor leaders, a 16-man 'revolutionary council' under General Hudson Austin, had replaced the elected government and assumed control. The island's main airfield at Point Salines had been closed to international traffic, a 24-hour curfew had been imposed on the civil population and violators were threatened with being shot on sight. In addition Soviet and Cuban backing of the regime was suspected by intelligence sources, who also felt that the lives of US citizens residing on the island were imperiled. A dangerous situation was developing and there was a real threat that the 1000 or so Americans in Grenada, including 600 students at the True Blue Medical School near Port Salines, could be held hostage. There was a further fear that the situation would escalate and that neighboring islands could be affected.

Recent intelligence source estimates as to the disposition and composition of possible enemy forces were vague. There were, however, obvious objectives which would have to be seized if the situation was to be brought under control. These were the release of the students at the medical school;

the freeing of the island's British governor, Sir Paul Scones; and the defeat of the Cuban and rebel forces on the island. The Americans had the military assets required to achieve all three aims, and troops were put on standby for a possible operation. A plan was prepared dividing the responsibility for the various vital objectives between the army, the navy and the Marines. Navy SEALs were to be responsible for the assault on the governor's residence and for the release of Sir Paul Scones who was being held there. The Marines were to conduct amphibious landings on the east coast, and capture Pearls airfield and the town of Grenville, while the army's Rangers would parachute into Port Salines. The latter objective was the most vital of the operation. The airport was close to the True Blue Medical School and was defended by a Cuban force which was in the process of constructing an extension to the runway.

Before the military operation could be effected a number of political factors had to be considered. The island was part of Britain's Commonwealth. The British were at that time unable to mount an invasion of the scale required to restore peace on the island but two Royal Navy vessels, HMS *Antrim* and RFA *Pearleaf*, joined the US

ABOVE: Heavily armed paratroopers await the order to move out during operations in Grenada.

Navy task force heading for the island. In addition a small complement of 300 men from the islands of Jamaica, Barbados, Dominica, St Kitts, Antigua and St Vincent, joined the task force. This consisted of nine vessels including the USS *Guam*, a special amphibious assault, command and control ship, equipped with CH-46 and CH-53 helicopters; the USS *Saipan*, a general-purpose amphibious ship carrying the 22nd Marine Amphibious Unit (22 MAU); and the USS *Independence*, a multi-purpose aircraft carrier with F-14 Tomcats, A-7 Corsair IIs and A-6 Intruders. The force was supported by additional aircraft, most notably AC-130 Spectre gunships of the 16th Special Operations Squadron, based at Grantley Adams International Airport on Barbados.

The US troops and their allies faced a combined force comprising 784 Cubans and around 1000 Grenadians. Most of the Cubans were construction workers and engineers, and included a number of women. However all had received small-arms training in Cuba and, in addition, there were more than 40 professional troops among them. Armed with a variety of small-arms the Cubans and the Grenadians were equipped with mortars and heavy machine guns. There were also at least six Soviet-built BTR-70 armored personnel carriers

which, with their 14.5mm cannon, were effective against both ground targets and low-flying aircraft.

The American invasion began in the early hours of 25 October, when a SEAL detachment took over the governor's residence without incident. Marines from 22 MAU landed by helicopter at Pearls on the other side of the island at about the same time and, after a brief firefight with Grenadian regular troops manning antiaircraft defenses, took possession of the airfield. Shortly after this, Rangers from the 1st Battalion were landed on the airstrip at Port Salines. The plan called for two waves. In the first wave the 1st Battalion was to jump in and secure the airfield for the second wave, comprising members of the 2nd Rangers, which would airland with the heavy equipment and vehicles. In the event the MC-130s of the 8th Special Operations Squadron came under heavy antiaircraft fire and only the lead elements of the first wave were dropped. AC-130 Spectre gunships were called in to deal with the antiaircraft guns and searchlights. Once this had been done the remainder of the first wave jumped in from 500 feet, an unusually low height at which reserve parachutes are useless. Within 90 minutes of the initial drop the Rangers had secured the airfield, the run-

BELOW: Grenadian and Cuban prisoners at Point Salines airfield before being moved out to a secure area.

way was cleared of obstacles and the first C-130 landed, closely followed by several UH-60 'Blackhawk' helicopters. As reinforcements from the 82nd Airborne Division began to arrive, the Rangers moved out and within an hour had secured the True Blue Medical School.

Fighting continued throughout the day. Navy and Marine ground-attack aircraft engaged enemy positions and key points across the island while gunships provided the advancing troops with fire support. Army and navy helicopters ferried paratroopers, Marines and Rangers around the island as they dealt with enemy resistance. A number of helicopters were lost to ground fire but overall casualties were remarkably light. The Marines' armor was brought ashore and the island soon came under US control.

The invasion of Grenada took the world by surprise and although there was much criticism of the action, many of the Grenadians thought of the American troops as liberators. The operation had achieved its aims. The threat to other islands in the area, from acts of subversion mounted from a Marxist-controlled Grenada, was confirmed by captured documentation. Intelligence

indicated support for the revolutionary regime by the USSR and North Korea, as well as Cuba. From the military standpoint the operation was a strategic necessity and, just as importantly, one in which America's elite forces succeeded in their assigned peacekeeping missions.

BELOW: Medics from the 82nd Airborne Division administer first aid to a casualty prior to his evacuation to a hospital ship lying off the coast of Grenada.

CONCLUSION

SINCE the American success on Grenada the future of a number of participating military formations seems more assured. Elite units such as those that comprise the various US special operations forces have often survived in fear of reductions in strength and budget, or of deactivation. Constant evaluations as to the benefits provided by organizations such as Delta, the Rangers and the Special Forces, are under scrutiny

RIGHT: A soldier of the 101st Airmobile Division prepares to rappel from the side door of a Black Hawk helicopter.

from military leaders, government and the people alike. Any operation, whether it culminates in success or failure, draws attention to the units involved, most of which would prefer to maintain a low-profile in keeping with the operations they are likely to be called on to undertake.

The success in Grenada, and indeed the failure at Desert One, have positive as well as negative effects. The constant evaluation these actions produce force both the units involved and their overall commanders to learn from the experience and to keep pace with changes in technology, tactics and likely threats. Elite military formations, especially those involved with conducting special operations, must stay ahead of the pack. The United States has now realized the importance of its various special forces and a joint special operations forces command has been set up, bringing elements of the army, navy and air force under a single command umbrella.

It is important to understand that the majority of units termed as 'elite,' especially those that are tasked with special operations, only exist with the help of regular 'conventional' forces from which they draw their recruits and which give them the firm base their activities require. Additionally, it should be noted that in order to operate these 'unconventional' units need the arms and services that provide the necessary back up. Marines need ships to transport them and their equipment. Amphibious landings require specialized craft and skilled crews. Airmobile troops must have helicopters and pilots, and paratroopers can only perform their missions with aircraft and aircrews. Without these material assets and their skilled operators, the elite forces described in this book would not exist.

BELOW: US Navy SEALs, seemingly happy both in and out of the water.

ACKNOWLEDGMENTS

The author and publishers would like to thank Ron Callow for designing this book, Maria Costantino for the picture research and Ron Watson for compiling the index. The following agencies provided photographic material:

Bettmann Archive, page: 52(left).
Bison Archive, pages: 1, 6(top), 14, 23(top), 25(below), 42, 61(top), 66(both), 67, 75.
Frank Spooner, pages: 2(top right), 72(top right and middle).
Imperial War Museum, page: 10(top).
Peter Newark's Military Pictures, pages: 16(top), 38, 52(right), 58(left).
Photri, pages: 2(below left and right), 3, 64, 70, 72(top left and bottom), 73(all 3) 74, 77, 78.
Rex Features/photo: Poveda 6(below), photo: Oxley/Poveda, 76(top), photo: Peter Carrette, 76(below).
Robert Capa/Magnum, page: 12.
Robert Hunt Library, pages: 4-5, 7, 15(both), 16(below), 17, 18, 19, 21(top left and below), 22(below), 23(below), 24, 25(top), 26(both), 27, 28(top), 32, 33(below).
The Research House, pages: 2(top left), 11, 68, 69.
UPI/Bettmann Newsphotos, pages: 22(top), 34, 36, 37, 39(both).
US Air Force, page: 20.
US Defense Department/Department of the Army, pages: 8, 13, 21(top right), 28(below), 29, 31, 40, 43, 44, 45(both), 46(both), 47, 48, 49(both), 50, 51(both), 53.
US Defense Department/Department of the Navy, pages: 54(both), 55, 56(bottom), 58(right), 59, 60(both), 61(below).
US Defense Department/Marine Corps, pages: 33(top), 57, 62(all 3), 63(all 3), 71.